# FIXING BUSINESS

# FIXING BUSINESS

## MAKING PROFITABLE BUSINESS WORK FOR THE GOOD OF ALL

## LORD DIGBY JONES

WILEY

This edition first published 2017.
© 2017 Digby, Lord Jones of Birmingham Kb

*Registered office*
John Wiley & Sons Ltd, The Atrium, Southern Gate, Chichester, West Sussex, PO19 8SQ, United Kingdom

For details of our global editorial offices, for customer services and for information about how to apply for permission to reuse the copyright material in this book please see our website at www.wiley.com.

*Library of Congress Cataloging-in-Publication Data is available*

A catalogue record for this book is available from the British Library.

ISBN 978-1-119-28739-1 (hbk) ISBN 978-1-119-28741-4 (ebk)
ISBN 978-1-119-28740-7 (ebk)

Cover design: Wiley

Set in 12/18pt MinionPro by Aptara Inc., New Delhi, India

Printed in Great Britain by TJ International Ltd, Padstow, Cornwall, UK

This book is dedicated to three special people:

To my Mum, without whom I guess I wouldn't be here! It is a privilege to help look after her at 93 given all those years she looked after me.

To my dear friend Simon Biggs who died too early in October 2016 and left the hole, where fun and laughter should be, that is always created when the bright flame of a life well-lived flickers out.

And most of all to Patti who over the past thirty-five years has been, is and God-willing always will be simply my rock.

# CONTENTS

# CHAPTER 1

# SOMETHING IS WRONG – AND IT'S EVERYBODY'S BUSINESS

*"As I grow older I pay less attention to what people say. I just watch what they do."*

—Andrew Carnegie

## WHAT'S THE PROBLEM?

One of the most important institutions in modern society is facing a shattering crisis.

In fact, the relationship between Business that is creating wealth and generating taxation, employment, products, services and innovations; government that is managing, regulating, seeking social progress, setting the rules under which everyone operates and has a mandate to lead, and society – all of us – is broken. That hurts everyone and it's something that should concern us all. Yet while the connection between politics, government and society is often reported and analysed, the crucial relationship between Business and society is much less understood.

We think we know about Business and, for the most part, we don't much like what we *think* we know. One of the biggest things that Business does is ultimately operate as the sole generator of taxation revenue for the country. When a Business makes money there are only three things it can do with the profit: reward the shareholders who took the risk by way of dividend or capital gain on sale, and the shareholder will pay tax on it. Or keep the profit in the Business, and pay tax on it. Or pay employees – who'll pay tax on it! That tax goes in part to pay the wages of people in the public sector – who'll pay tax on it! If it wasn't for the wealth created by Businesses across the land, large and small, there would be no tax, there would be no public sector. It's the same with pensions. No Business, no public-sector pensions because of the tax revenue that pays for them. No Business, no private-sector pensions because of the salaries and wages that pay for them.

This lack of understanding and misrepresentation has some serious consequences. The few headline-grabbing, self-fulfilling prophecies endorse our prejudice and allow us to assume that the Business of wealth creation is an entirely selfish activity carried out by untrustworthy rogues, and that anyway Business is just where the money lies; cash is king and nothing else matters. As a result, we are quick to penalise Businesses and executives, and slow to give them any benefit or support.

Business faces a range of difficult problems – many of its own making, some that are not – and it is time that these were addressed. Fundamentally, Business has to recognise that it has a vital role to play in society and it needs to start fulfilling that role better. This book is about Business: what it

> **A business that makes nothing but money is a poor business.**
>
> **Henry Ford**

means, why it matters and, more significantly, the challenges it currently faces and the solutions that it needs to adopt if it is to succeed for the benefit of us all.

We are concerned about a "democratic deficit" – the need for people's views to be reflected by the politicians that serve them – yet we seem unconcerned about (or perhaps we are simply happy to accept) a "Business deficit". If Business continues to detach from society, then both Business and society will, in many ways, be much, much poorer.

Fixing Business matters hugely. This book is written from a UK perspective but the points it makes will resonate wherever you live in the world and many of the examples cited are international. The role of Business in our society and lives is truly global, more than ever before in human history. Gary Clyde Hufbauer of the Peterson Institute for International Economics highlights the fact that virtually all of the "losers" of the 20th century rejected international economic links, either explicitly (in the case of the old Soviet Union) or implicitly (most of Africa). Whereas the "winners" of the 20th century embraced the international economy, for example: Japan, Korea, Taiwan, Spain and Ireland. In virtually all of these cases, the economic development and trade driven by Business contributed to stabilising entire societies, many of whom had previously endured turbulent times. Finally, those countries that have grown and prospered the most in the 21st century have accelerated their embracing of the global economy; Chile, Vietnam, Mexico, China and India spring to mind.

This point will be especially relevant, in 2017 and 2018, in the UK. As we discuss later in this book, it underpins the opportunity provided to the UK by Brexit, the country's departure from the European Union. The UK wants, among other things, more direct control of its trade and the opportunity to complete trade deals with other parts of the world. Other current members of the European Union may aspire to this too. Clearly Business and trade matter, and they are exerting a remarkable influence on political developments.

The most significant challenges and much of the mistrust facing Business are universal – just look at the rise in recent years of anti-globalisation protests – and the opportunities and remedies that Business leaders need to adopt are largely universal too (although the context may vary). This point about globalisation is complex but it does also serve to highlight the complexity of Business. Business is predominantly a force for good and so too is globalisation. And where there are problems with Business (and globalisation) they need addressing and resolving, not ignoring, pretending they don't exist or rejecting everything that they have to offer. It is, in part, fear of the effects of globalisation, whether perceived or real, that created the energy that powered Donald Trump to the White House. Millions across the developed world feel, rightly or wrongly (as if there can be an objective "right" or "wrong" about this) that globalisation works for the few not the many. Business had better face up to that reality or the consequences will be dire.

One other vital point is worth highlighting: Business and commerce are not alien or inherently unusual activities, they naturally spring from the human condition. We make things, we provide services, we trade, we compete and we work to improve things, not despite the fact that we are humankind, but because of it. Creating wealth through Business has always been with us and, like it or not, it always will be. The key, therefore, is to make sure that it works better than ever before – and why wouldn't we? There are few engines of progress and change as potentially beneficial as Business. This means that Business is here to stay; it is inevitable and a crucial part of who we are and what we do. That may be an uncomfortable truth for some people; one of the biggest drivers for people is the desire to do well. Many of the greatest innovations and successes in human history have been driven by commerce and Business: from the discovery of the New World in the 15th century to the dramatic improvements in healthcare achieved in the 20th and 21st centuries.

Consider these few facts: the global population at the start of the Christian era has been estimated at around 150 million people. It reached its first billion people in 1804, and by 1900 was 1.6 billion. Between 1900 and 2000 the global population nearly quadrupled, from 1.6 billion to 6.1 billion, and between 2000 and 2011 it increased by a further 900 million to 7 billion people. In other words, there was a bigger net increase in global population in the first 12 years of the 21st century (900 million) than the entire growth in global population between AD1 and the year 1804 (850 million).

The extent of the changes in global population that have taken place during our lifetime is astounding. This point is highlighted by the 20th century, which was particularly remarkable. During the last 100 or so years there has been the highest annual population growth rate (2% in 1969) and the shortest time for the global population to double, which it did between the administrations of US presidents Kennedy and Clinton.

This was combined with unprecedented declines in mortality, changes in healthcare, education and incomes, significant international migration and increased urbanisation, resulting in the emergence of mega-cities. According to the United Nations, in 2007 the global urban population exceeded the global rural population for the first time in human history.

The post-second world war era has seen enormous strides in the improvement of standards of living across the globe. Global average real incomes per head rose 460% between 1950 and 2015. Over the same period, the proportion of the world's population in extreme poverty fell from 72% to 10%. The global average life expectancy at birth was 48 in 1950; by 2015 it had risen to 71. These are some encouraging statistics which often get lost in the din of the doomsayers.

Business is one force, but a significant one, among several that are constantly shaping our world. From the opportunities in the cities to the internet that creates feelings of awareness, aspiration, envy or resentment, Business has been the driver for the greatest economic migration of peoples the world has ever seen.

## WHAT HAS BUSINESS EVER DONE FOR US?

So, what precisely are the main benefits of Business? Why are we so certain that it is worth the effort of fixing? Well, let's spell it out. Here are just a few of the indispensable things we get from Business. National wealth, distributed throughout society by corporate taxation and used to improve society; employment; communications; improvements in healthcare leading to longer lifespans and better quality of life; pensions; education and training; cheaper food and with greater variety; support for local communities; economic development for poorer parts of society and the wider world; technological innovations – from tablets and smart phones to electric cars, wind turbines, television and air travel; trade, leading to greater understanding and connectedness with other societies; environmental protection; plentiful energy; cultural developments – from sports teams to film, art and entertainment; infrastructure; water; security; personal financing; housing; fashion and clothing, transport and travel. The list goes on.

You may object to some of these but all of them, to a greater or lesser extent, were invented or at least innovatively brought to market by Business drivers, and all of them need Business if they are to work effectively. If you doubt this then consider those examples of societies, such as the 75-year history of the Soviet Union, which believed capitalism and Business to be obsolete ways to deliver anything. As it turns out, they were very badly wrong.

If that was not enough, there are also many intangible, personal and valuable psychological benefits of working in a commercial enterprise. I am no psychologist but it seems clear that, for many people – although admittedly not everyone – feelings and needs such as purpose, loyalty, fulfilment, affiliation, pride and competitiveness are all addressed not simply by working, but by working together in a commercial competitive environment. It is worth repeating that Business is here to stay: it is a crucial part of who we are and what we do.

The challenge, therefore, is to get politicians, the media and, crucially, society at large to be more supportive of Business as an activity – wealth creation – that profoundly benefits society. What is needed is a view of Business that is more objective, balanced and fair, and this can only be achieved if Business people are prepared to take the initiative by putting their heads over the parapet and explaining the good stuff they do.

It is worth asking the question: why are Business people so resented and reviled? Populist politicians and the media perpetuate the problem, constantly giving people bad news stories that distort public perceptions of Business. The truth is that Business is a reflection of society and – like every other part of society, for example, the church, politics, police, armed forces, media, the civil service – Business employs a vast majority of decent, diligent, well-intentioned, hard-working people alongside a small minority of rogues and scoundrels. Yet it is those rogues that get all the attention and this even extends into popular culture. For example, every time a "baddie" is needed in a film or television soap or drama it is invariably an unscrupulous Business person. This crucial point is often misunderstood: Business is not a nameless, faceless entity; it is entirely made up of people, mostly good, sometimes not. Yet if any other group in society were picked on as thoroughly and relentlessly as Business executives there would, quite reasonably, be concerns expressed about fairness and the potential harm caused by constant vilification. The difference is that Business is an easy target. Its occasional mistakes are amplified and seized upon while its contributions, successes and achievements are ignored, and there are too few people willing to make the case for Business.

This is not a whitewash though: Business clearly has problems and attitudes that need fixing, and they need fixing for the good of Business. One of the main problems (that actually gives rise to many others) is that some Businesses fail to recognise that people do not like to feel controlled, manipulated, abused or simply disregarded, even if it is only their perception. In other words, Businesses needs to get better at doing their job: showing leadership, connecting with people and being accepted in the communities where they operate.

This principle is best highlighted by a personal story. This one is mine but I guess we all have a similar tale we could tell. I feel powerless when dealing with BT, my telephone provider; if the bill is incorrect or something goes wrong with the service then the effort to get it fixed is so enormous that my resentment is building before I even start. My thinking is this: why don't you make dealing with me easier? And if that takes more money then put me, the customer, ahead of the profit for the shareholder.

The usual sanction open to me in a commercial world is that unless I get the level of service I expect, I don't pay … except this is not available to me in my dealings with BT. If I refuse to pay until my problem is sorted, then I will be cut off. If I do what they insist and pay, then I have no leverage (and they have no incentive) to fix anything. The only option available is the nuclear option of leaving them. This creates a feeling of resentment, of being abused, to the point where I think, "What is the point of even looking at the bill?" To make it worth looking will mean I have to enter into a ghastly labyrinthine world of complexity, hanging on, delay and frustration. And therein lies the rub: BT would possibly reply that they have millions of customers and a huge and complex service to deliver. Process and technology are their areas of focus. My point is this: if you can't provide a genuine service, one where you make each individual customer feel better and special, then you have failed. In BT's case, and possibly many others, this might mean that the Business has simply become too big.

I have concluded that a lot of resentment directed at Business and what people think it means to them comes from their experiences with Businesses that deal remotely with them. The individual feels powerless and abused by the Remote, All-powerful Call Centre. It is often based overseas and (it might be politically incorrect to say so but it is the reality) the consumer often cannot understand what the person is saying, is already fed up by the patronisingly insincere, "How are you today?" and thinks, "I'm paying for this!" Mobile phone companies, energy Businesses, banks … all find themselves regularly at the top of the "I hate Business" list and all charge for the delivery of … er … apparently anonymous, omnipotent poor service. These companies claim that they must keep costs down and that the consumer is unwilling to pay for a more personalised, less automated service. How about trying them? And what if the additional costs were not passed on to the customer but ate into the profits instead? Isn't it a price worth paying by shareholders for a better general view of capitalism and thus the greater chance of survival of the system which gives shareholder returns in the first place? Of course, a reduction in the big pay cheque for the boss would also help in the perception war as well, if not in reality when spread across the entire cost base.

## HARNESSING A POWERFUL FORCE FOR GOOD

Businesses exist to make money, that's the way it works and it is a positive force that drives Business. It's positive because making money requires Business to understand that the customer comes first, second and third. Making money relies on the customer and that is the essential driver of productivity, efficiency and innovation. Second comes the employee: the person who helps you serve customers and make money. Third comes the system – an ever-changing situation. To succeed, Business must be constantly flexible and dynamic, constantly up for change.

Contrast this with the public sector: the system comes first. "We don't do it like that round here" is the public servant's cry. A close second are the people who work in it. Highlighting this point is the view of many socialist MPs that parts of the public sector, from the NHS to Britain's nuclear submarines, are there for the jobs they create ahead of the benefit that the tax payer is seeking.

The third priority in the public sector, and it is a poor third, is the tax-paying customer. The subliminal message to the customer is: "Put up with it, it's free." This is not a call for privatisation: it is a call for changing the ethos in the public sector. A focus on customers means a focus on service and efficiency, disciplines that improve the value we receive from our public sector. Invariably it is the pressure of the market that drives productivity, service and innovation.

Crucially, what drives people is people; the desire to do better than someone else, and to compete; something that socialists too often overlook. That is simply what people are like; it is an essential part of the human condition; anywhere, everywhere and through time. Or, to put it another way, the only way to slow or stop this competitive instinct for progress and success is with totalitarianism through prison or at the end of the barrel of a gun.

Business is in a unique position to blend the natural drive of people wanting to better themselves and make money, with the standards and values we all hold dear. It helps to temper people's drive to compete and succeed so this is productive – but not always. It is the same drive that creates our best Business executives and some of our worst. So, the challenge for a twenty-first century Business and the people who lead it is to channel that drive for the benefit of everyone: customers, employees and society as a whole.

## GETTING TO WORK: THE PROBLEMS THAT NEED FIXING

So, let's look at those areas of vital importance that should be addressed by Business if they are going to win back hearts and minds. These are the problems that need fixing, issues that we will look at in more detail in later chapters.

First, the problem of Business reputation and branding. Let's all agree that the reputation of vast swathes of Business is a disaster and at an all-time low. Vitally important for wealth creation, tax revenues, education, employment and for everything we want to achieve as a society, the health of Business should matter to everyone. So, in a globalised economy that in many ways runs on credibility and confidence, it matters that institutions as large and significant as corporations are disliked and distrusted.

Take banking as an example. Since at least the time of Shakespeare, the reputation of bankers and money-lenders and the affection in which they are held has never been very high, but since the financial crisis of 2008 the feeling in large parts of society has been that "bankers" are untrustworthy, selfish and greedy at best, and unremittingly evil and rapacious at worst. They devastated the economy and profoundly affected such crucial issues as interest rates, property prices and the amount of money available for social services. Even today it seems as though it will be a long time, if ever, before their reputation can be restored. Yet financial services employ millions of honest, decent, talented and hard-working people worldwide, and the work they do is vital; enabling people to buy homes and provide for their families and their future, and helping Businesses to trade, employ more people and grow.

## There is a Tax, and There are Attacks

Financial services is a global industry in which the UK excels. Crucially, it generates a huge amount of tax for the UK. Approximately 11% of total UK taxation comes from financial services. According to the consultancy PwC working with the City of London, the UK financial services sector in the year to 31 March 2015 "paid an estimated amount of total taxes in the region of £66.5bn, or 11.0% of total UK Government tax receipts". In addition, employers' National Insurance Contribution is the largest tax borne at 33.5%, and 1.1m people (3.4% of the UK workforce) were employed by the sector. PwC estimates that financial services companies pay £25,439 on average in employment taxes *for each employee.*

Given these facts does it really help constantly to criticise, ridicule and undermine the sector? Should our attitude not be more positive and constructive? Financial services is an intensely mobile global sector, and if we keep telling people they are not welcome then they could just make Dubai, Mumbai or Shanghai's day. "Beware what you wish for because you might just get it" has never been more apposite.

The issues facing the sector are framed almost exclusively in terms of how we can curb the excesses, not how we can support the industry. Clearly the problem arises when you see huge bankers' bonuses being paid, or colossal salaries for average performance, and quite understandably that is what people see, rather than the good that they do. So two things surely need to happen: bankers need to get their house in order (regulation clearly has a valuable part to play in this but bankers need to do much more as well), and society needs to stop screaming at them and adopt a more constructive attitude. Continually shouting at a recalcitrant child is not only very bad for the child, it isn't great for the parent or family either. Find a better way.

There has been an increase in the intimacy permitted by consumers to characterise the relationship between them and businesses that sell them what are increasingly seen as essential services. Digitalisation, social media, and the creation of a world modelled by Bill Gates and Steve Jobs have diminished face-to-face communication. Conversations have all too often become unilateral exercises in assertion or a route for the shy or aggressive to "have their say", and through the conventional social intercourse traits of face-to-face contact or instant reactions. The branded device has become irreplaceable, a comfort blanket, an opiate of the masses for the 21st Century. But such insidious power, such brand reliance brings huge responsibility. The huge threat to societal and job security of constant, unceasing disruptive technological advance imbues correlative responsibility on the perpetrators to ensure their fellow human being is not left behind. The bigger and better your brand, the more customers and society expect from you. Which is at least part of the reason why the legal but unpopular tax avoidance tactics of firms such as Google, Amazon, Facebook and Starbucks are so incomprehensible to so many people – and potentially harmful to these firms.

Surely Facebook "get it" when their 2014 sales revenue worldwide was $12.5bn, with UK revenues of £105m and the firm claiming that a third of UK adults visit their site every day, and yet the firm paid just £4,327 in UK corporation tax. This was because they made an accounting loss of £28.5m in Britain in

2014 after paying more than £35m to their 362 staff in a share bonus scheme. In fact, in 2014 staff at Facebook's UK Business took home an average of over £210,000 in pay and bonuses. I find it incredible that a Business that relies so much on the goodwill of its customers is not thought of badly for exploiting this situation, and for not making a substantially greater contribution to the society that generates their income. Socialists claim that "making tax-avoiding multi-nationals pay their fair share of tax" will somehow provide all the increased revenue the Exchequer requires. It is a seductive argument. What I fail to understand is how the same members of the public who cheer the vilification of such corporations actually do nothing about it themselves; surely the Amazons and Starbucks, the Googles and Facebooks, would respond to a customer boycott far more speedily and meaningfully than any ponderous government initiative? But the inherent double standard of the consumer is constantly exploited … and the result is then wrapped up in anti-Business bile by the very people who won't take action themselves!

One of the most important benefits of Business is obviously pay and employment and all that this brings. This not only includes intangibles such as progress, stimulation, satisfaction, esteem, confidence and fulfilment but other more down-to-earth benefits: greater skills, education, pensions and employability, for example. These skills and benefits actually work for the good of everyone, enriching the whole of society. Having a workforce that is highly trained and effective makes our Businesses more competitive and our economy stronger, and the careers of those skilled people are more secure, better paid and more rewarding.

We should also recognise that education and training address one of the biggest weaknesses of the UK economy: the need to enhance productivity, both in terms of hours spent and capital invested. The best way to do this is to skill and train our people better and in more depth and breadth every day: from abolishing adult illiteracy and innumeracy to substantially improving the quality of management.

Finally, people with some skin in the game of their future, where through being skilled they can choose what to do rather than just be done to, make for a safer and more understanding world, richer in the pocket and richer in the soul.

**Protecting the environment.** The undoubted fear and one of the most potent criticisms of Business is that it trashes the environment. It does this, so the argument goes, by, for example, using energy to manufacture or trucks for transportation. And when it comes to producing and selling energy *that* is worst of all: coal is unclean, gas is a fossil fuel contributing to global warming, renewables such as wind turbines blight the beautiful countryside and nuclear energy has unacceptable risks and perilous waste products. In fact, the environmental issue highlights the broader problem facing Business: it is too easy to criticise and condemn Business but there is no recognition that enterprise is simply providing what society wants, needs and expects. It is meeting a market need for things like food and energy coming from all of us. Criticising Businesses because they give you what you want is hypocritical and foolish. There has to be a better way.

And there is. Effective regulation operating alongside Business helps ensure that free enterprise prospers and provides us with what we want and need, while at the same time curbing harmful or unwanted practices. But if ever there was an area where globalisation could be harnessed to effect real change it is here. Business cannot fix this one on its own; it is a global problem.

**Understanding and fixing the issue of executive pay.** Consider this: in the UK if you set up a Business, risk money that you cannot afford to lose, work and sweat harder than you ever have before, employ people, sell a popular product or service, put your personal life on hold, build a successful Business, pay tax and, eventually, are able to afford a luxury car, you will probably be regarded as a greedy, flashy and probably unpleasant individual. Whether from fear, jealousy or sheer envy people will think negatively of you. Whereas if you win the lottery people will smile, wish you well and, probably, think positively of you.

There are two key issues that matter when it comes to wealth and pay: did you earn it, and what have you done/are you doing with it? I know a great example of a hugely talented executive who built a world-class, market-leading Business, a major public company, from scratch. It took him all of his professional life and, several years ago, it was agreed with the shareholders that he would receive total remuneration (including shares) of £70 million if he met certain agreed targets relating to turnover, profit and dividend. All of the targets were achieved, his leadership and results were superb, and so he took the £70 million package to which he was entitled. Because the targets had been met all of the shareholders benefited, which would almost certainly include millions of other people (you and me) through our pension schemes. So, what's the problem? The point is this: at a time when there are so many low paid but highly skilled people feeling that they deserve more, yet unable to receive large pay rises because the nation can't afford it, surely here was a marvellous opportunity for a talented Business leader simply to set a better example and very publicly take much less simply because he could.

It is in situations like this that the reputational battle will be won or lost.

You may argue that executive pay is an issue of personal freedom, and it may be, but there is a bigger and broader issue

**"A very rich person should leave his kids enough to do anything, but not enough to do nothing."**

Warren Buffett

here as well that Business leaders often forget. Executive pay is a leadership issue. Restraint and reasonableness matter, because to do otherwise is to disconnect from people and reject a leadership role, a role which has helped you achieve your wealth in the first place. A sense of entitlement undeniably undermines Business and that negatively affects us all. This contrasts with leadership, which undeniably strengthens Business and society and benefits us all.

**Bridging the gulf between big Business and small businesses.** There's no way to hide this point or dress it up: too often big Business can behave terribly, for example, by using their size and purchasing power to bully and dictate terms to smaller suppliers. There are just too many examples when small firms are used as banks by their larger customers. Supermarkets, for example, receive the goods and sell them often on the same day, and then take over 90 days to pay their supplier. Why? Well, the time value of money is one reason. By taking 90+ days to pay their bills they can invest and use the cash they have already received. Meanwhile the smaller Business is struggling to finance its own costs. The big boys unilaterally change the terms of Business with their suppliers, taking longer to pay simply because they can. Each change is only a small blip for the large company, although cumulatively it matters, while it can mean corporate life or death to the small supplier.

This situation is not only grossly unfair, it is actually counter-productive for the big Business. They are missing out on their suppliers' genuine loyalty and the benefits of a close, associative partnership – such as flexibility, innovation and quality – instead reducing everything to a win/lose squeeze on margins and costs. Part of the solution is proper, enforceable regulation (probably with some form of criminalisation), part is informal "naming and shaming" of big Businesses and part is a better understanding of the benefits of genuine partnerships in a supply chain.

> **Rank does not confer privilege or give power. It imposes responsibility.**
>
> **Peter Drucker**

Finally, there is a national issue here that should concern us all. By taking an unreasonably long period to pay their supplier, the big Business is robbing the smaller supplier of the chance to invest in training, plant and equipment or expansion – because the small Business is having to use all its cash and ingenuity simply to survive until it gets paid. Do you want to expand efficiency and employment in the UK economy? Then help small Businesses get paid more quickly and in a way that is fair and reasonable.

**Doing the right things, right: corporate social responsibility.** Business would often benefit from much greater genuineness and an improvement in the way they exercise their leadership role and influence. Too often firms come into a community, for example, and spend money on a worthwhile initiative so that their Business or brand will be given greater affection or achieve a higher profile. Profile and the pursuit of affection are not, by themselves, sufficiently compelling reasons to do good. Businesses should do good simply because it is the right thing to do – and many Businesses understand this, although their efforts are largely unreported. Acts of corporate social responsibility (CSR) may help benefit their Business understanding, or motivate and engage their employees, or provide some other Business benefit, but that cannot be the sole driver and reason why something is practised. CSR is practised because Business contributes to society, and every enterprise needs to be genuinely accepted and welcomed in the places where it does Business. True, genuine CSR does not reside in someone's in-tray or in a department; it truly only works when it is in the DNA of the entire Business and everything that it does.

Connecting all of these challenges are the things that are needed to Fix Business:

- **Business should shout about what it does that is good for society.** Business leaders need to get on the front foot much more, reassuring and explaining to people that the Business of wealth creation is not only exciting, honest and worthwhile, it is essential.

- **A balanced media,** one that explains and celebrates the incredible progress being achieved by Business, not only exposing bad practice and behaviour.
- **Courageous, insightful politicians** who stop paying lip service to the need for wealth creation and start actively defending, supporting and encouraging it. I learnt a long time ago never to listen to what politicians say, but rather to watch what they do.
- **Genuine leadership and a clear understanding of their role from Business executives and entrepreneurs.**

Wishing for these things to happen is not enough, practical action is needed and it is Business that needs to take the initiative. This need for action starts with the battle to restore the reputation of Business, the issue that we explore in the next chapter.

## Key Questions

- What are you and your colleagues doing to enhance the reputation of Business in your community? What more could you do?
- What, where and who are your community?
- Do you have regular two-way dialogue and sharing with local schools and colleges regardless of the size of your Business?
- What has been your Business's greatest success in changing lives for the better? How widely is this known and understood?

- In the absence of good news and engagement the media may find bad news, or none at all. So, how well – and how frequently – do you engage with the media?
- How easy is it to attract the best employees to your Business? What more could you do to make your Business genuinely attractive?
- Do you work up and down your supply chain on issues relating to CSR, skills and training and media liaison?

# CHAPTER 2

# WHERE THE BATTLE IS BEING LOST: FIXING THE REPUTATION OF BUSINESS

*"It takes 20 years to build a reputation and five minutes to ruin it. If you think about that, you'll do things differently."*
—Warren Buffett

## WHAT IS WRONG WITH THE REPUTATION OF BUSINESS?

It is hard to think of a time when the reputation of Business was worse than it is today. It is disastrous, and it really matters.

Perhaps the first thing to say is that Business and its leaders can be their own worst enemies. Often there is too little leadership, or Business is too quick to focus on profit or process, apparently at the expense of customers and wider society. There are very few Business people who would not consider themselves as being professional in what they do, yet one very good definition of a professional is someone who puts the interest of their client or customer ahead of their own. I would suggest that this is a definition that would not suit too many Business people. It is understood by the general public almost subliminally and respect is the first casualty; teachers many years ago and, more recently, junior hospital doctors fell foul of this loss of professionalism in the public's eyes and their standing has never recovered. Business, sadly but too often deservedly, is seen in the same light.

**One very good definition of a professional is someone who puts the interests of their client or customer ahead of their own.**

Undeniably, and perhaps surprisingly, Businesses are sometimes slow to announce progress or success, partly because they may worry about putting their head over the parapet, partly for competitive commercial reasons and partly because they do not feel that branding or publicity matters. In fact, there is a range of serious, genuine and concerning reasons why the reputation of Business is so tarnished. How often do we see routine examples of Business treating ordinary customers badly, or simply providing a quality of service that the Business itself would hate to receive? It amazes me that someone somewhere in the Business isn't saying, "Would I like to be treated like that?" The consequence is that Business falls into the prejudiced maw of politicians who relish the opportunity to give capitalism a good kicking. One train company that isn't doing at all well translates into, "Nationalise the lot!" As if running a train operator from the floor of the House of Commons would make for a better railway, or changing the recipient of profit from Business risk-taker to tax-payer would make the politically motivated trades unions accept, for the first time in recorded history, change through the adoption of technology.

There are bad apples, corporate deceit, foolishness and inefficiency, and these combine to feed an anti-Business firestorm fanned by a gleeful press and politicians, both of whom recognise an easy, populist way to boost their own agendas when they see it. This misses two vital points, however. First, Business needs to get its own house in order: the Business of wealth creation is not only intrinsically decent and honourable and something that can bring out the best in us all; it is, more importantly, essential. Remember, it is in the DNA of all of us, it is a basic human instinct. Second, a cynical "glass half empty" view of Business does no one any favours. All of us in society need to develop greater interest in and respect for the achievements of Business and the people working in Business.

**Doing the right thing doesn't always bring success. But compromising ethics leads down the road to failure.**

Let's just take one example: the rise of China's economy since 1980 and its boost to global trade is not only the greatest poverty reduction exercise in history, it has also provided us all with an opportunity to trade and prosper. Trade is not a zero-sum game; rather, it enriches us all. There may have been many complex, sometimes negative reasons for a vote in support of Brexit, but I prefer to focus on the positive opportunities it provides for Business; notably greater trade with countries like China. If we can fix the undeniable reputational problems with Business then we will be left a clearer and more powerful force for good. India, America, Australia, Brazil: all are waiting for Business to get stuck in and make the most of greater trading freedom for the UK, resulting in more profits, more UK jobs, and more UK tax income.

So, what are those problems?

## There are Bad Apples ...

"It is hard to see an upside in the demise of British Home Stores ... with more than 11,000 employees. Sir Philip Green bought the business ... for £200 million in 2000. He and his family received £586 million in dividends, rental payments and interest on loans before he sold BHS for just £1. This is the dark side of capitalism: increased borrowing and payment of ever bigger dividends; risk transferred from the private to the public when the business fails; the low paid and the taxpayer left to pick up the bill … Sir Philip, the king of shops, has led a life that would put Louis XIV to shame … acquiring three super yachts … the BHS pension fund fell from a surplus of £17 million in 2002 to a potential deficit of £571 million today …" wrote the Right Honourable David Davies MP in the *Financial Times.*

There is no evidence that Sir Philip did anything illegal but politicians rarely miss such an open goal when it comes to making the poor behaviour of the few tarnish the reputation of the many. A thousand Businesses may do great work but the reputation of all of them is easily and instantly demolished by the actions of one or two rogues or idiots. Sir Philip eventually, commendably, made a voluntary contribution of some £365 million to the BHS Pension Fund but the damage to his reputation had been done a long time before and that is where the battle was lost.

This is no excuse, however. Business leaders need to show leadership, first and foremost, demonstrating the standards they expect of their people and instilling in all their employees the values and standards that should apply, always. Crucially these standards must, of course, meet the minimum expected by their stakeholders and the wider society.

In 2016 the UK Parliament's Business, Innovation and Skills committee questioned Mike Ashley, the entrepreneur and owner of retailer Sports Direct, who participated in the committee meeting reluctantly and under duress. Parliamentarians heard evidence that his employees were afraid to take sick leave in case they lost their jobs, leading to 76 ambulance call-outs in two years and one employee giving birth in a toilet. As if that wasn't enough, some of the practices, such as excessive docking of pay for lateness and lengthy after-hours searches, are said to have left employees effectively earning less than the minimum wage. "It seems incredible that Mike Ashley, who visits the warehouse at least once a week, was unaware of these appalling practices," committee chairman Iain Wright MP said. "This suggests Mr Ashley was turning a blind eye to conditions at Sports Direct in the interests of maximising profits, or that there are serious corporate governance failings which left him out of the loop in spite of all the evidence." In the global unpopularity contest between politicians and Business executives, which must be a fairly difficult race to win, it seems that the executives are in the lead.

## ... There is Corporate Deceit ...

A different example of the type of damage caused to the reputation of Business is provided by the German carmaker Volkswagen (VW). In September 2015, the United States' Environmental Protection Agency (EPA) found that many VW cars being sold in America had a "defeat device" – specially designed software in diesel engines that could detect when they were being tested and change the car's performance accordingly to improve the test results. The German car giant has since admitted cheating emissions tests in the US.

VW had undertaken a huge marketing campaign in the US to sell its diesel cars, trumpeting the vehicles' low emissions. The EPA's findings covered 482,000 cars in the USA only, but VW has since admitted that about 11 million cars worldwide are fitted with the so-called "defeat device".

According to the EPA, VW's engines had computer software that could sense test scenarios by monitoring speed, engine operation, air pressure and even the position of the steering wheel. As a result, when the cars were operating under controlled laboratory conditions the device appears to have put the vehicle into a "safety mode", with the engine running below normal power and performance. Once back on the road again the engines switched out of this test mode. As a result of this trickery, VW's diesel engines emitted nitrogen oxide pollutants up to 40 times above what is allowed in the US.

VW's response was the admission by the group's chief executive at the time, Martin Winterkorn, that his company had "broken the trust of our customers and the public". Mr Winterkorn resigned as a direct result of the scandal and was replaced by Matthias Mueller, the former boss of Porsche, who said: "My most urgent task is to win back trust for the Volkswagen Group – by leaving no stone unturned." Presumably this will be after he has changed the ethos of the company, away from a culture which actually paid clever people to develop software with the specific aim of cheating. Until that deep-rooted characteristic is sorted out the external campaign to win back the trust of other stakeholders will be meaningless.

VW is paying up to $10,000 in compensation to each customer in the USA but is refusing to pay any compensation to British and other European owners. They are also dragging their corporate feet in rectifying the problem in cars within the EU. According to *The Times* in December 2016, Greg Archer, the clean vehicles director at the campaign group Transport & Environment, has said: "VW is operating above the law in Europe with feeble government regulators afraid to act against this corporate cheat." A spokeswoman for VW has responded: "There is no compensation for owners outside the US because the relevant facts and complex legal issues that have played a role in coming to the agreements in the US are materially different from those in Europe."

So far as recovering a trashed reputation goes, and so far as a new management regime being seen to do the right thing is concerned, this is such an appalling response as to deliver at a stroke every self-fulfilling prejudice held by every anti-Business lobbyist. It would appear that VW are not compensating owners of their cars in Europe to whom they actively lied … just because they can! They are forced to do it in the USA so they do; they are getting an easier ride in Europe so they don't. Whatever happened to doing the right thing; not just saying sorry but showing by their actions that they mean it?

*The Times* reported that VW says it has written to 500,000 customers offering to fix the problem (presumably for free!) and, of those, 295,000 had responded and had the work done. "It was unable to say," reports *The Times*, "when it would invite the other 700,000 customers with affected cars." You invent software with the specific intention of deceit, you advertise your products with knowingly spurious data as a selling point, you get caught and then … ?

VW has since launched an internal inquiry, recalled millions of cars worldwide and set aside $18.3 billion to cover the actual costs of the emissions scandal. They agreed in June 2016 to pay $15.3 billion in partial settlement of just some civil claims in the USA. Fines, penalties and criminal prosecutions will follow on both sides of the Atlantic; a $4.3 billion penalty in the USA was agreed in February 2017, and individual indictments will follow. The long-term reputational costs of the scandal, however, are beyond estimation.

## … and There is Inefficiency and Foolishness

My cousin received a letter from a bank … except that the letter was not meant for her: it was addressed to her recently deceased husband. The bank knew he was deceased because after his name on the envelope it included the words "(deceased)". And they were writing because she had been in the branch only a few days earlier and expressly asked for all communications to come to her, not her late husband. At that meeting the bank had commiserated, sympathetically helped her into her new banking relationship, even changed their system while she waited in the branch so she could see what was going on – and then wrote to him anyway!

This may seem like a "one-off" but there are many examples of call centres, letters, communications and Business practices that are inefficient, incorrect, downright unintelligent (who writes to someone who is deceased?) and offensive. This folly is compounded by the behaviour that we frequently see from corporations that disappoint us or simply miss our expectations. Bank branches are inconveniently closed, our ability to contact a Business is limited or difficult, pricing is unintelligible, service is poor … the list goes on. To add insult to injury we, the consumer, are often told that a specific measure which increases our sense of inconvenience and remoteness is being done "to enhance the customer experience" or "create a more efficient service level", when in reality we all know that the description "to increase our profits" (and, by unfortunate deduction, the decision-makers' bonuses) would be nearer the mark. Of course, increased profits do mean increased dividends and increased share prices for all those whose pension funds have shareholdings in these companies (virtually all employees, present and retired, public and private sector, do) but that important irony is lost on the frustrated, upset, exhausted consumer … and the reputation of Business suffers.

## This Feeds a Firestorm of Hysteria that Damages the Good as Well as the Bad

The anti-globalisation protest movement resulting from these actual and perceived excesses is spreading. Widespread and disparate, protesters coalesce around a concern about political, economic and social exclusion and a perception that governments are not ensuring that corporations act in a socially responsible way. Seen as wielding massive power, corporations are now expected to change the way they do Business. Protesters' tactics include direct action, legal redress and brand-bashing publicity.

Political commentator Noreena Hertz highlights several forces now arrayed against large corporations that affect their ability to attract employees (over 50% of university graduates would not consider working for an unethical Business). These forces include:

- **NGOs (non-governmental organisations).** People trust NGOs, such as Greenpeace, and their campaigns are now increasingly effective and focused on corporations. The watershed came in 1995 following a high-profile action by Greenpeace with Shell reversing their decision to dump the Brent Spar oil platform in the Atlantic Ocean.

- **The actively angry.** This group lashes out as the gap widens between "haves" and "have-nots". They apply direct action and seek legal redress. Legal campaigns focus on corporate compliance with norms of international law and matching standards of care in operations abroad with the standards expected at home.

- **Grass roots activists.** They are brand-bashing, creative, often humorous and always unpredictable. They chiefly use film, posters and the internet to ridicule brands.

- **Governments,** which are expected to address environmental, social and ethical concerns. Their likely response is regulatory. Indeed, if governments responded to every demand, then every single activity in Business would be forbidden!

Business has too few people willing to understand, recognise and celebrate the good that it does and the value it generates for us all, and too many who are quick to jump on a bandwagon of righteous disapproval and point out its shortcomings. One intensely disappointing incident that I experienced first-hand illustrates the formidable challenge facing Business as it tries to get a fair hearing in the court of public opinion. It occurred when I was at a press lunch in Birmingham where the guest speaker was the popular and renowned journalist Robert Peston. Towards the end of the Q&A discussion I asked Robert a question: "It's five minutes until the Six O'Clock News starts, a story has suddenly and unexpectedly been dropped and the editor needs from you a single business story. All other things are equal and there are two stories you can choose between: a good news business story and a bad news business story. Which one do you go for?"

"That's easy," he replied. "The bad news business story."

"Why?" I asked.

"Because I'm not a f***ing cheerleader for business!" was the damning reply, in front of hundreds of people. You're clearly not, Mr Peston, nor should you be, but a bit of balance would be nice!

## WHAT IS THE ANSWER?

There has been an increase in the view that Business brands are corporate tools designed to grab our attention and manipulate our wallets, rather than being valuable, reassuring guides to the type of products and services we would welcome. A sceptical public also misses another key point about brands: the blend of distinctiveness, familiarity and reassurance that they provide is valuable to their firms. Brands are increasingly valued on companies' balance sheets as they provide a source of loyalty and competitiveness. A brand may be trying to appeal to you, or it may not be for you at all, but these are not reasons to assume that they are innately manipulative or harmful. Businesses themselves, however, too often fail to appreciate the responsibilities that a great brand bestows. The bigger and better your brand, the more that customers and society expect from you. Which is at least part of the reason why the legal but hugely unpopular tax avoidance tactics of firms such as Google, Amazon and Starbucks are so incomprehensible to so many people, and potentially harmful to these firms.

I asked an audience at an event why so many people still use Facebook if they are so disappointed with that firm's approach to tax avoidance. Why is it that people don't vote with their feet and go elsewhere if the Business they use behaves in a way that they dislike by avoiding tax? The answer from one woman surprised me: "Because they are my friends." Surely it is not right that Facebook exploits such unquestioning goodwill. This level of loyalty places on Facebook a huge moral responsibility, one that they are clearly not discharging as well as they might.

Such loyalty and affection for firms is not new, and it's easy to understand why. People in general are social beings: they particularly like to connect and affiliate with other people and groups. So, in the context of people as employees and customers they value dialogue, connection, service and, as a minimum, they expect respect and they expect their employer or the firm with which they are transacting to do what they say they will. In fact, in the 21st century expectations for greater dialogue, decency and connectivity have increased as quickly as the technology which drives them.

Executives at Facebook might answer that the only responsibilities they have are to deliver returns to their shareholders (and delivery of a great product and service to their customers is Route One to that) and to respect the norms of society (in other words paying the tax that is required – tax avoidance, not evasion). Therefore, it is, of course, down to the governments of the countries in which they operate to change the rules and address the issue. We're not looking for the norm, we are looking at what needs to change and how to fix things. So, in the case of Facebook and their tax, the best approach is simply to suck it up: if you are serious about changing the reputation of Business (and your enterprise in particular) then you just have to pay. Then you can be proud of the change: people will see you are playing in a way that is fair and sincere and governments will cut you the slack you need. But there is no silver bullet: you need all aspects of this to be aligned, and therefore it is reasonable to expect Robert Peston to report that good news story too.

One thing that we should not lose sight of is the conflict facing individuals – a consequence of Business that will, in my view, always persist. It works like this: Mr Smith works at a local supplier to Sainsbury's. He wants Sainsbury's to pay as much as possible for his employers' goods. But he shops at

Sainsbury's so he wants Sainsbury's to pay as little as possible for those goods. He then wants Sainsbury's to pass on that saving to him as a customer but, as a shareholder of Sainsbury's through his pension fund (and most of us are), he wants them to keep the saving to enhance dividend-boosting profits, not pass it on to the customer at all. This triangle of conflict is insoluble and yet is the source of much anti-Business grievance. Perhaps for improved understanding the solution is not continually or unreasonably to complain, but instead see the connections and decide which of these various roles (consumer, employee or shareholder) matters most, and to what extent.

## Show Ethical, Strong and Consistent Leadership

**"Treat others as you would want to be treated." This simple rule surely applies in every aspect of life and it certainly applies in Business.** Whether the issue is individual or corporate malpractice the answers are clear and consistent: first, show leadership by doing the right thing and behaving ethically, always. Any doubtful ethical behaviour should be rooted out. Corporate governance needs to be effective but it is no substitute for genuine leadership; the kind that inspires people always to do the right thing.

Business sometimes forgets that it needs to be accepted in the places where it operates. For example, Americans are rightly outraged by the way a German carmaker has treated their country's environmental standards.

It is worth noting that costs of $18 billion are only part of the penalty being paid by VW for the emissions scandal. Arguably, the greater long-term harm is caused by a damaged market reputation, sagging future sales, a decline in the firm's share price and increased difficulty in recruiting the right people – all of which are huge reasons for Businesses to get it right.

## Regulate

Clearly, governments are expected to address environmental, social and ethical concerns, and their likely response is regulatory. In fact, an increase in regulation also extends beyond governments to supranational bodies such as the European Union. These institutions have steadily increased regulation in areas such as corporate governance, data protection and employment.

This gives rise to two problems: first, if you can't regulate uniformly in a globalised society then commercial activity will gravitate to the more lightly regulated society. The opportunity to create wealth at home for the benefit of all society is thus diminished by unavoidable participation in a globalised and competitive economy. For example, in 2002 the United States introduced the Sarbanes-Oxley Act requiring CEOs formally to vouch for the accuracy of their firm's accounts, with draconian personal penalties if they didn't. This had the effect of driving a great deal of commercial activity and its tax generative benefits away from America.

The other problem with regulation is that it can frustrate and curb the essence of wealth creation, with innovation put in the "too difficult" box and the appetite for risk fast disappearing. This is highlighted by the situation facing the Financial Services sector. For all its sins, and there have been many, ultimately it is the consumer who will pay for a Financial Services sector that is buried under the destructive weight of excessive regulation. Indeed, those who still carry the torch for the UK remaining in the European Union seize on any news of a bank reducing its London presence as evidence of a negative reaction to Brexit, whereas the reality is that excessive, over-reacting regulation, messianically implemented, is suffocating the lifeblood out of UK-based banking.

Clearly, there has to a happy medium. Without regulation, market failure (a characteristic of any capitalist economy) and events of unconscionable exploitation of customers, shareholders or both will recur and reach damagingly high levels. In a post-banking crisis world, it does look as if cautious and electorally sensitive politicians are allowing the pendulum to swing too much one way.

## Monitor and Measure what Matters

It really is the case that what gets managed gets measured, and what gets measured gets done (in the words of the writer on management issues, Peter Drucker). So, Businesses need to measure the things that matter to them – their customers and the people connected with the Business; those things are rarely unit sales or the accumulation of wealth for shareholders. Of course, choosing the best measures depends on the size, history and nature of the Business, but information and trends relating to speed of response, delivery times, cost efficiency, measures of customer satisfaction, customer issues or complaints, as well as other vital issues such as the time taken to pay suppliers or the amount of effort spent on training, are often (if not always) vitally important.

Measurement matters because managers should not just be looking at the issue, they should be seen to be focusing on it. That way everyone's attention is directed to the issues that matter, and people outside the Business, such as current and potential customers and employees, can see the Business's intention and priorities.

However, measurements need to be accurate and revealing. Be objectively critical and ask: are you measuring the right things, and how can measures be improved? And then, most importantly, don't just say in response to findings or events which embarrass you, "lessons will be learned." Show your customers, employees, suppliers and the media that you have done something about it: explain what has been done in the necessary level of detail. It is worth remembering that while people may not like receiving bad news, it is preferable to receiving no news at all.

## Develop a Reputation for Ethical Behaviour

Several universal personal attributes are fundamental to ethical behaviour. These attributes include: integrity, competence, honouring confidentiality, transparency and an ability to recognise conflicts of interest and act appropriately. These are so significant that it is worth considering each attribute in detail.

### Integrity

This includes being honest, avoiding unprofessional behaviour and possessing a responsible regard for the public interest. In practice, this means checking the reliability and accuracy of information before dissemination and never knowingly misleading people: "Doing The Right Thing". I remember having this explained to me very illuminatingly when I was Director-General of the Confederation of British Industry by a chairman of one of my major member companies, who called it the "*Daily Mail* Test". Would you like to see your actions, words or behaviour on the front page of the *Daily Mail*? If you would not, even if what you're doing is legal, don't do it.

### Competence

In practice, this simply means attaining an acceptable standard and, ideally, being good at what you do. It also means being aware of personal limitations, and working to develop and improve one's personal skills. In a leadership role it means being willing to collaborate and delegate, but never asking someone to do something they know you wouldn't do yourself; accepting the loneliness of leadership, accepting responsibility and being publicly the "last on the bridge".

## Honouring Confidentiality

Respecting confidences, avoiding the use of confidential or inside information either to secure an advantage or to disadvantage someone else and never disclosing confidential information without specific permission, either to protect the public interest or where it's required by law. The key is to tell a client: "I would never say anything confidential I know about you to anyone else. But in return, I will never tell you anything that I know about someone else that is confidential." That way, your integrity and honesty are understood and respected.

A great practical example of this approach was provided by Joe Beattie MBE. After serving in the British army Joe joined the Downing Street driving corps where he drove several British Prime Ministers, before leaving and joining the CBI as the driver of the Director-General. As the newly-appointed DG of the CBI I had the pleasure of being driven by Joe Beattie, and soon after I started I remarked, curiously and invitingly, "You must have some stories to tell about the people you have had in the back of your car over the years."

Joe's response was polite but firm and absolutely correct. He explained that he wouldn't ever tell anyone about what he'd heard while he was driving me, and he would not be telling me or anyone about anything he heard while driving someone else. No gossip, no sense of self-importance, no shallow or misguided attempt to ingratiate himself with his new boss. Just a firm, honest and decent belief that something told or heard in confidence should be held in confidence, forever. At a time when sharing information, news or stories is easier and more tempting than ever, Joe's approach is both impressive and reassuring; the epitome of professionalism.

### Transparency

Being transparent in the way you do Business means recognising conflicts of interest and acting appropriately. This involves conforming to accepted Business practice and ethics, for example, by disclosing any financial interest in a supplier. It is a sad fact of professional life that often, when faced with a conflict of interest, acting in the honourable way diminishes your short-term financial return. And therein lies the temptation to which, too often, good people succumb.

## LISTEN AND UNDERSTAND: COMMUNICATE EFFECTIVELY

One vital technique that is much maligned and misunderstood but extremely valuable in helping to connect with people and prevent reputational damage is public relations.

## The Principles of Great PR

PR is about dialogue, not control. Unlike other related activities in the area of sales and marketing, PR does not control its messages. It is about influencing, an activity that requires dialogue with the public. This dialogue occurs through multiple channels and the result is a perception that builds into a single brand.

Closely related is the fact that great PR engages with people instead of avoiding or ignoring people or their issues. The key to success is to engage – even when things aren't right and especially if there are problems or concerns. PR is about relationships with people who agree and disagree and this requires relationship-building, a positive two-way discussion, and the ability and willingness to ensure that the top team are on board with the key messages.

**God gave you two ears, two eyes and one mouth. Use them in proportion ... Too many people are in "transmit" mode, not receive.**

This leads to another important principle: PR needs to be strategic and actively supported by senior leaders. Clearly, the messages that an organisation sends out have to be genuine and consistent which is why they need the support of executives at the very top. Senior executives not only need to understand and believe what is being said, they must also ensure consistency and appropriate action throughout the organisation.

Several other issues spring from the strategic nature of PR. First, it requires internal support as well as an external focus.

Communication, dialogue and understanding are as important within an organisation as they are outside, sometimes even more so. Also, PR involves continuous change, improvement and an ability to make tough choices. Changing and improving what you or your organisation does is an essential aspect of PR. After all, PR is about building relationships and from time to time these require action as well as listening. An interesting example is provided by the public interest in the UK in 2009 over the expense claims of members of parliament. In this instance listening to and understanding public concern was simply not enough: behaviours had to change and improvements needed to be made.

This highlights another important truth about PR: disclosure is essential. The example of MPs' expenses and the concerns about corporate activities that gave rise to Sarbanes-Oxley legislation, for instance, show that you cannot manage relationships with the public and disclose information *selectively*. Not only is disclosure usually the ethical thing to do, it is also the most sensible, given that technology and globalisation will converge to ensure that a message given at one particular time and place to one group will spread to other groups at other times. The truth is that MPs should have been applying the *Daily Mail* test (or, in this case, the *Daily Telegraph* test, as this was the newspaper that carried, on a daily basis, lists and details of the abuses of the parliamentary expenses system by our parliamentary representatives) much, much sooner.

## Technology: Creating and Improving Relationships

Another way to address the reputational difficulties facing Business is with technology. Technology is there to serve you, not the other way round, but too many people are slaves to technology rather than using and applying it on their own terms. A useful example is emails between people working in the same office: intended as an aid to communication, email can have the opposite effect, killing communication and stifling other methods which have developed over millennia – like chatting. The real problem with emails is that they are unilateral. They don't readily allow an exchange of views, they can be ignored, they can land at the wrong moment or be absent at the right one, and they are often missing the context or depth that comes from an exchange in person or on the phone. Of course, they are brilliant as well in many situations but they have limitations.

Technology is continuing to shape public relations in profound and far-reaching ways, providing both opportunities and threats. In particular, technology is transforming the way that people access, find and use information. People can now gain access to an unrivalled range of images, information, knowledge, people, products and views through Twitter, YouTube, Instagram, Facebook, blogs, podcasts, the internet, apps and a myriad of other technology-based services. In these circumstances the traditional role of PR professionals as media gatekeepers is changing profoundly. Because of technology, the challenges of PR and "reputation management" affect a much larger number of people in a Business than ever before.

Above all, technology is affecting the way that organisations engage in dialogue, build relationships and connect with people. Audiences have become much more capable and savvy with all types of digital media and PR has to evolve with them. Gauging and influencing public opinion requires an ability to use online media – and this can include individual blogs. There are now many more potential influencers who need to be recognised and considered.

One of the priorities for PR professionals is to harness the potential offered by social media. Clearly this is an indispensable part of Business, but there are two problems. First, the people leading our companies tend not to be part of the social media generation – although this will obviously change over the coming years, hopefully quickly. Crucially, those people making decisions about communications are not skilled and may be quite fearful.

Second, social media companies are not doing enough to reassure or help protect their customers from abuses of the system. Social media companies need to develop a reputation for not tolerating abuse, and for ensuring that every miscreant troll or hacker fears the full force of the law for their actions. Social media companies need to be socially responsible, working with society to bring abusers to justice.

It doesn't stop there: we all rely on Wikipedia for information, and while it is undoubtedly a fabulous and inclusive creator and disseminator of knowledge, it is also open to abuse. It is curated and edited by ordinary people: most entries are great, some are not. Many a mischievous (or worse) factually inaccurate entry is planted on a page but is accepted as "gospel" by a naive consuming public. Wikipedia is not a verified scholastic work of reference! As a result, expensive verification and constant monitoring is an industry in itself, which is surely an example of the law of unintended consequences.

With social media, a distinction needs to be drawn between what is useful and what is froth. "Creating a storm on social media" is not always a bad thing: it can excite, engage, inform or rightly hold to account those that deserve criticism. The question to ask, therefore, is who is causing the storm, and for what purpose?

Clearly, social media is a valuable, vital tool because it facilitates dialogue and brings the openness that is at the heart of successful PR. Openness and transparency not only result in good public relations, they matter because they enable people to build trust, reputation and support. The difficulty with this is the same as with any relationship: it requires a genuine commitment and positive regard for the other person or people. In short, it needs effort. Social media requires us to establish trust, rapport and dialogue. This is achieved by what you say, what you do and what others are inclined to say about you. In fact, restoring the reputation of Business lies in the ability to recognise this simple truth and act accordingly.

The challenge of restoring the reputation of Business also relies of course on the other areas, and it leads to one key question: how can the Business of wealth creation be (and be seen to be) a better force for good in society? That, after all, is one of the great shifts we have seen in expectations about Business, especially since the turn of the last century. It may not be a simple or easy question to answer but it forms the focus for the next chapter: achieving socially inclusive wealth creation.

## Key Questions

- Are you measuring the right things; the things that really matter to your customers and people?
- How well does your organisation listen to its stakeholders and people who care about, or are affected by, its Business?
- Where are the risks in what you do? Where is your Business vulnerable to criticism, and what can you do now to address or resolve this?

- Who are your key constituents and how can you improve your dialogue and relationships with them?
- Do your senior executives understand how to communicate with people outside the Business, recognising the need for dialogue with key constituents?
- Do the people who manage your reputation and branding (such as public relations professionals) have access and support at the highest levels?
- Do your communications strike the right balance between telling and listening?
- Do your communications recognise the challenges and opportunities of globalisation and technology?
- Above all, is your organisation open and sincere with its communications? Does it adopt an ethical approach? Does it always mean what it says and do the right thing?

# CHAPTER 3

# ACHIEVING SOCIALLY INCLUSIVE WEALTH CREATION

*"Surplus wealth is a sacred trust which its possessor is bound to administer in his lifetime for the good of the community."*

—Andrew Carnegie

## TIME TO RETURN TO SOCIALLY INCLUSIVE WEALTH CREATION

If the reputation of Business is to be restored, then far-reaching changes are vital. As we have seen, getting a fair hearing is important; so too is avoiding the excesses, foolishness and bad behaviour of Business, and creating an environment where

Business can thrive and perform at its best. When this happens wealth and employment are created; taxes are paid to fund society's priorities; products and services are developed and delivered which enrich all our lives, and economic security is firmly established.

Even so, that's not enough.

It is not enough for investors to flourish while tough, vital decisions are made without any consideration for the people and communities that provide the employees and, in many cases, the customers of the Business. More needs to be done, and it has been done before. The answer is to ensure that wealth creation – Business – is socially inclusive. By that I mean that it is seen to include a wide section of society, treats those people with dignity and respect, is acknowledged as being a force for good because it is seen as taking everyone with it and being there for everyone; it recognises not only that it pays off to include people and share the benefits of Business, it is also, quite simply, the right thing to do.

This was the approach that began in the early days of the Industrial Revolution, when some enlightened industrialists built factories in rural locations and then provided housing for workers clustered around the workplace. This continued throughout the 19th century. An early example of what became known as the model village was New Lanark, built by Robert Owen. Philanthropic coal owners provided decent accommodation for miners from the early 19th century. Others were established by Edward Akroyd at Copley between 1849 and 1853 and Ackroyden in 1863. Titus Salt built a model village at Saltaire, and Henry Ripley, owner of Bowling Dyeworks, began construction of Ripley Ville in Bradford in 1866. Industrial communities were established at Prices Village by Prices Patent Candle Company and at Aintree by Hartley's who made jam, in 1888. William Lever's Port Sunlight had a village green and houses with an idealised rural character. Perhaps most memorably of all, the Quaker industrialist George Cadbury built Bournville, a model village, beside his factory between 1898 and 1905.

When George Cadbury began building his factory at Bournville in 1895 he did so, not as a single-handed attempt to solve all of Birmingham's social problems, but in the hope he could prove that good quality housing in a natural, green environment – something that he felt was a necessity for the greater good of society – was Route One to a healthier, more productive workforce who felt more valued. He challenged the thinking of the day and sought to change current attitudes by practical example. This was leadership in the raw.

Sir Dominic Cadbury says that when his grandfather, George, went the extra mile to care for his workforce, building houses and providing schools and better working conditions, he was always one step ahead in his thinking: "You could argue that the vision of the man was so remarkable that it was unthinkable that government would ever have to come in and tell George Cadbury what to do. George Cadbury was telling the government what to do and leading society."

Now isn't that a good lesson for Businesses who complain about too much government interference? The impact of forward-thinking industrialists from Andrew Carnegie to George Cadbury can be dismissed as being irrelevant in the modern age, but in my time as Director-General of the Confederation of British Industry I often looked at Cadburys (and other successful Businesses run on similar lines) and wondered why, given how they provided clear evidence that you can successfully link social inclusion and wealth creation together, more Businesses hadn't done it. For many people, several crucial questions need answering before they embrace socially inclusive wealth creation. Those questions include:

- Why would industrialists do this? Why spend the money on socially inclusive wealth creation?
- Is this not patronising and anachronistic in the 21st century?
- What is the best way to achieve socially inclusive wealth creation today?
- What drives an entrepreneur?

It is worth pausing to understand why we are in Business at all. The answers to this question are many and varied. For example, some people have few options, others inherit, others have a burning passion, but I would argue that underlying all of these motives is the nature of our humanity: for many, many people it is simply who we are. Since the time of the cavemen we have had a need to provide for others, and we have evolved to compete as well as collaborate, to make and sell as well as to want and to buy. A whole range of factors make us commercial animals, and making money and serving customers results in a strong sense of achievement and satisfaction that we find rewarding. But these commercial animals are *human*, which means, by and large, that we are also hardwired to care about the people around us. Not necessarily all of them, but not usually none of them! We are social animals with a love of friends and family and frequently a passion for our community, society and country as well. The simple truth is that if there is an opportunity to improve that society further then many Businesses and their employees will happily take it.

And this is nothing new.

Highlighting this fact and providing at least part of the answer to the questions highlighted above is the example of another great industrialist, Weetman Pearson.

## THE PEARSON STORY

In most organisations, people wish to leave it a better place than when they arrived: they aspire to deliver quality as well as achieve recognition and reward. This should come as no surprise; after all, very few successful people are content simply to work on a pointless endeavour for long. Proving this point is Pearson, the largest education company in the world with some of the strongest brands in Business information and consumer publishing, including Longman, Penguin and Pearson itself; for many decades it was also the owner of the *Financial Times (FT)*. Senior Pearson executives go out of their way to explain to their managers how the Business started, how it has come to be successful and what makes it special. This in turn helps people understand and appreciate Pearson's culture and values – and it's an inspiring, instructive story.

Weetman Pearson was born in July 1856 in Yorkshire, in the north of England. His grandfather Samuel started the firm known today as Pearson in 1844 and for many years the firm focused on construction, eventually becoming one of the world's largest construction companies with most of its operations outside the UK.

Aged 17 and having already run one of his father's Businesses in England, Weetman Pearson spent a year in the USA in 1876. It was a formative experience that prepared him well for building the world's largest construction company, as well as laying the foundations for today's Pearson. Impressed with America's infectious energy and enthusiasm, Weetman Pearson came to learn two lessons that are as relevant today as they were in the past: don't ask people to do things you would not do yourself, and treat others as you would like to be treated. He took this advice to great lengths, physically helping to construct some of the projects then being built by his company. These exertions left him in hospital more than once.

An early supporter of globalisation, Weetman Pearson took over the company in 1880, at the ripe old age of 24. The Business that he developed built Dover harbour as well as railways and major civil engineering projects around the world. In 1889, Porfirio Diaz invited him to Mexico to build a railroad from the Atlantic to the Pacific. While laying track, his crew discovered one of the world's largest oil fields, the Potrero del Llano. He created the Mexican Eagle Petroleum Company, one of Mexico's largest firms. It was taken over by the Royal Dutch Petroleum Company (now Royal Dutch Shell) in 1919.

After 1918, Pearson bought several newspapers and it was these, together with his values and approach to Business, which laid the foundation for the company of today. He treated his employees with care and generosity, understanding that people needed to be encouraged and directed if they were to give their best. Uncaring, unthinking brutality at work would be ultimately self-defeating. Of course, this is a concept about Business that civilised societies have come to understand and now enshrine in law, but in Weetman Pearson's world of the 19th and early 20th centuries – and in the rough world of construction – it was quite a departure from the norm. For example, he was the first employer to provide his workers with pensions and he also believed in employee share ownership.

Pearson would have had many people from the "establishment" of the time criticising, obstructing and opposing his ideas, whether openly or behind the scenes. It did not matter: Pearson's approach was, quite simply, the right thing to do. Unlike personalities in the media and politics, working in Business should not be a popularity contest. With the challenge that wealth creation brings comes responsibility: not just responsibility to manage risk and deliver for customers, innovate, treat employees well and so forth, but also a wider leadership role in society. Of course, I could sell it to you on the basis that it's good Business, but the bottom line is that if it is good for people and society then it is good for Business in a way that is sustainable, reputation-enhancing in the long-term and building up understanding and goodwill, even if there is little or no short-term reward.

Combined with Pearson's international approach was a strong sense of entrepreneurship, commercialism and values. It mattered to Pearson that his Business was being built on a firm set of principles. Weetman Pearson understood that it is possible to be honourable, honest and profitable. After serving as a Member of Parliament, including a spell in the wartime government of David Lloyd George in 1917 where he was responsible for aircraft production, Pearson eventually retired and died in May 1927. His obituary highlighted his 'daring, originality and ingenuity', while his own philosophy emphasised perseverance and patience. All of these qualities remain hallmarks of today's Pearson.

> **What matters most is not simply what the company does, or its size or even the company's output, vital though these things are. What matters to its employees and, ultimately, its customers, is *who it is*.**

From the 1960s onwards the company that Pearson had built began to focus even more on publishing, eventually growing into one of the world's most successful publishers. This shift from one industry to another may seem strange but it is by no means unique – other major corporations such as Nokia have similarly shifted their focus (in Nokia's case, from timber to mobile telephony). Pearson's story suggests that what matters most is not simply what the company does, or its size or even the company's output, vital though these things are. What matters to its employees, its shareholders and, ultimately, its customers, is *who it is*. Weetman Pearson was certainly not a saint, but anyone who hears the Pearson story being told cannot fail to be impressed by the tale of a brave, enterprising, visionary and decent young man who simply enjoyed his work and let his personality shine through. Ultimately, he gave the company the character and culture it has today, a character that seems to have survived for more than a hundred years and has spanned a diverse range of industries, countries and challenges.

Pearson executives today use the story to remind their managers of the company's character and values: for Pearson, these are to be brave, imaginative and decent. Now, many firms espouse high-minded values that can seem to their employees to be vacuous, but set in the context of a past that includes Weetman Pearson's priorities and style, and a present position as one of the world's largest publishers and education Businesses, these values have real meaning to people at Pearson. This is how one of Weetman Pearson's legacies – the firm's values – were described in 2009, 82 years after his death:

- **Brave and daring.** Being willing to drive forward with energy and determination is vital. Bravery also means doing things you never thought you would do. You need to *dare* to make progress, sometimes even to do the right thing over the status quo or pressures of others.
- **Imaginative.** This is what Pearson is all about: connecting with people and being thoughtful and creative in all that we do.
- **Decent.** People at Pearson should follow Weetman Pearson's example and treat others as they would wish to be treated. Being decent also means erring on the side of generosity.

Pearson succeeds by giving real meaning to the work of its employees. Today, for example, the company is hugely proud of the fact that it is working in Angola to produce textbooks in seven indigenous languages for many different communities, some of which have never previously had a single textbook. This isn't simple altruism: the firm employs 30,000 people worldwide and has made steady returns for its shareholders, despite sometimes challenging economic circumstances. Of course, the firm will inevitably make mistakes and do the wrong thing from time to time, just as a person might (because only you and I are perfect!), but it's character that counts and that can be shaped by the past as well as leadership in the present.

Is it just coincidence or happenstance that a company with this character and history – one that is tirelessly and proudly handed down from one set of managers to the next – is also a leader in the highly competitive Business of educational publishing? Surely it is much more likely that this corporate character is attracting talented and enthusiastic people, inspiring and engaging them so they can truly excel and, ultimately, deliver great results (and not only commercially).

The equation is simple: for the most part, companies such as Pearson have an ethos and approach that gives meaning and value to their work; people (mostly employees) respond, and the Business thrives. Making this happen in practice is, of course, the challenge of leadership.

This also highlights another important truth about the way Business is done: sometimes genuine mistakes will be made and accidents will occur. That is in the nature of life and it certainly applies in Business. One should often judge a Business, therefore, by how they deal with the mistakes that they will inevitably make, perhaps by asking the questions: was their intention positive? Do they act quickly and responsibly? Business deserves to be met halfway by society. A significant example of this point is provided by the BP response to the Deepwater Horizon tragedy. BP established a fund to help local communities immediately, to prevent delays resulting from legal battles so that the impact of the tragic disaster would be quickly mitigated for local communities along the Gulf of Mexico. This was eventually abused by many spurious claims, from phantom Businesses and phantom losses. More than 100 people were jailed for making fraudulent oil spill claims against BP; 311 were convicted with 102 sent to prison, 7 receiving sentences of 5 years or more and 1 person got 15 years! So, even though BP acted responsibly and did the right thing they were abused by society. In these circumstances Business people could be forgiven for thinking "Why did we bother?"

## ACHIEVING SOCIALLY INCLUSIVE WEALTH CREATION

Several practical actions are needed if Business is going to take the radical steps needed to rebuild trust. These ideas about the challenge of achieving socially inclusive wealth creation were explored in detail by me in a BBC Radio 4 programme in August 2015.

## Establish a Business Covenant

The first point is to remember that there has been a breakdown in trust with Business, one that is going to be difficult to repair. To fix things we may need a new deal for Business – a covenant – setting out in simple terms where the obligations for Business lie and what it can expect in return from the government. I think a Business covenant should be loosely based on the military covenant which has been around for years as an unwritten moral agreement between the armed forces, society and government.

It states that in return for sending servicemen and women into harm's way, government specifically, and society generally, will look after them and their families. This principle has, in fact, now been enshrined in law.

I don't want to burden Businesses with yet more laws or regulation, so my Business covenant is more of a mission statement for UK PLC. Here it is:

*Business creates the wealth on which the nation depends. The government commits to supporting Business through providing an environment in which it can flourish, including infrastructure and an educated workforce.*

*Business, in turn, commits to society through investment, job creation, fair treatment of its workforce, customers, suppliers and shareholders and through the payment of taxes.*

*Through its deeds, Business will establish, enhance and promote the existence of quality social capital in the communities of our nation as well as the economic capital that only it can develop.*

It sounds like common sense but sometimes the obvious needs restating.

## Recognise Your Moral Duty

The Very Reverend David Ison, Dean of St Paul's Cathedral, says that a covenant is more than a contract, it's a commitment, and he believes it could express a Business's obligations to a community: "You want to see business saying, 'Yes, we are committed to the life of this locality. We have a commitment to the people here and we recognise our responsibility to them.'"

But he says this is often not the case: "One of the things which people have found very difficult is the way that business appears to be able to uproot itself and say, 'We're not making enough profit here, we'll close our factory and move somewhere cheaper.'"

A Business covenant would be a commitment, like an agreement sealed with a handshake.

Clearly Businesses have to take difficult decisions for commercial reasons. But while they are not charities, walking away from the social consequences of their actions goes against what the Business covenant is about.

Justin King, the former chief executive of Sainsbury's, believes Businesses have a moral duty to go beyond what is expected of them. "I believe it's the things that businesses do that they don't have to which define where they sit in society," says Mr King. "As a citizen, we would not consider someone who says, 'I just obey the law, no more,' as a good citizen. That's a base-line level, I would suggest. I don't think corporations are any different."

Justin King argues that every Business should pay its fair share of tax and has no time for those that avoid doing so, even when this is within the law as it stands for some international companies. But how many of us complain about well-known Businesses which don't pay their fair share of tax while continuing to buy their products?

To restore trust in Business, Mr King believes companies must also do things for society, which have no obvious short-term financial return.

This belief is clearly shared by David Morley, the out-going Senior Partner of Magic Circle high-earning City law firm, Allen & Overy. He founded Prime, a group that tries to give legal work experience to people in the UK from disadvantaged backgrounds.

## Be an Agent of Social Inclusion

Small Businesses are often, by their very existence, agents of social inclusion that are contributing to the local community. They pay taxes, provide services and support, and employ people locally. Interestingly, they are rightly angered and often disappointed by those larger Businesses that do not always value or take seriously their connections with local communities.

Encouraging Business is vital: Business reflects society, good and bad. Of necessity it involves risk and reward and includes the very real possibility of failure, or at least fortunes falling as well as rising. This is a truth that is ignored, misunderstood and simply not tolerated by socialists. Making wealth creation socially inclusive is vital, but if Businesses' actions and motives are constantly hammered then you will simply not get investment in tomorrow's drugs, or any other life-enhancing product. Our response to Business should be more encouraging and reasonable; if, when Business succeeds it is either taken away by unreasonable amounts of income tax or by social denigration, then society's problems will become much worse. That, surely, was the example provided to us for 75 years by the Soviet Union. A truth about the human condition is that creating wealth is a norm; if by excessive regulation (so it goes in the too-difficult box) or penal taxation (so it really isn't worth the effort or it's worth taking one's hard work or innovative ideas to other countries and creating wealth there instead) or by threat of imprisonment or worse you diminish or extinguish the wealth-creative drive, then every single person (and especially the poor) suffers.

## Changing Eating Habits

The developed world has now reached the point where many of its poor are not thin, they're obese. It has become often cheaper to eat out (and badly) than eating in.

The medium to long-term impact on the cost, to us all, of the NHS can be lessened by there being fewer obese and unfit people. Yet many Businesses are providing them (and making money from doing so) with the very food and drink that causes the problem.

"We live in a free world" is a fair enough cry and "moderation in all things" is a counsel of perfection. But would it not be one up for Business in its battle to fix its reputation if it were seen to do more in the realm of health education insofar as it concerns diet, and if it were to seize initiatives before being made to act by the threat or actual implementation of regulation? The contribution to the future cost of healthcare provision would be immense and the obvious innovative talent of the Businesses facing the challenge would surely find solutions to mix the "naughty but nice" with the "good for you" competing maxims.

## Giving Credit: The Five Taxes Business Pays

### Understanding One of Life's Certainties

We have already said that Business does not get enough credit for the good that it does, but when it comes to contributing to society's wealth and assets directly, through taxation, the gap in understanding is even greater. Every small Business owner in the UK knows what tax they need to pay, and in jurisdictions outside the UK there are very similar taxes to these five. However, relatively few people outside Business appreciate the scale of Business taxation, and the costs of administration borne by the Business needed simply to calculate the amount of tax due, pay it and have it subsequently verified.

**Income tax.** If you are a sole trader, you pay income tax on your Business's profit. Assuming you don't have any other income, such as salary from a job, as well as what your Business makes, then you'll start paying income tax on your Business's profit once it goes over the personal allowance. If your Business is a limited company, you could pay income tax on any salary or dividends you take from the company. If you do not take income from a limited company then income tax will not be paid, but if that money represents profit then such retained profit left in the company will be subject to Corporation Tax.

**National Insurance (NI).** Although not strictly a tax, it might as well be given it has the characteristics of taxation (pay up or else). National Insurance (NI) is paid to the government so it is often referred to as a tax. It was originally established in the UK to fund the National Health Service. Sole traders pay two kinds of NI: a flat weekly rate of Ni called Class 2 NI (unless your Business's profits are under the Small Profits Threshold. Class 2 NI is currently £2.80 per week). You will also pay Class 4 NI once your Business's profits go over a certain level (currently set at £8,060). Class 4 NI is worked out as a percentage of your Business's profit.

But it's when Business starts to employ people that NI's pernicious effect takes hold. Crucially, NI is a tax on job creation. No basis in profits or income: if a Business is losing money but employs people, it still pays NI. Profit is only used as the benchmark to calculate how much a Business pays. It is significant that when Patricia Hewitt was the UK Secretary of State at the Department of Trade and Industry, she famously said that NI was going to be increased in the Budget for employees so it was only fair that it also went up for "the Bosses"! How utterly, demoralisingly wrong and muddle-headed: an employee only pays NI if money is earned; a Business pays NI if a job is created, regardless of money being earned or not. And there's another important point here: the boss is a person, an individual, whereas NI is paid by the employer. Patricia Hewitt was trying to create the impression that employers' NI was paid by a rich individual running a Business and employing people, whereas the reality is that such a person is also employed by the Business and pays employee's NI, while the Business is creating the jobs and paying employer's NI. Sadly, the Secretary of State was trying to personify a corporate tax insidiously raised and jokingly hypothecated and to capitalise on anti-Business sentiment.

**Corporation tax.** Limited liability companies pay corporation tax on their profits. There's no equivalent of the personal allowance for limited companies, so as soon as a company makes any profit, unless it's previously made losses, it will start paying corporation tax. Currently in the UK this tax is 20% of profits for all companies, and it's payable nine months and one day after the company's accounting year end. Sole traders do not pay corporation tax.

**Value Added Tax/VAT.** This tax highlights the point that Business is a huge, totally unpaid and administratively burdened tax collector. No matter what kind of Business you have, sole trader, partnership, LLP or limited company; if your Business makes VATable sales above a specific threshold (currently £82,000 a year) you have to register your Business for VAT. The current standard rate for VAT in the UK is 20%.

**Business rates.** If your Business operates from office or retail premises, then you may have to pay Business rates; this is like a property tax, but for Businesses. In October 2015, the government announced that, by the end of this Parliament, local authorities will be able to keep 100% of the Business rates they raise locally. This is a fundamental change to the way local government is financed.

Many other taxes – such as a levy on banks – are also paid by specific Businesses. Little wonder, perhaps, that the accounting profession in the UK and elsewhere is thriving, and will hopefully raise awareness in town halls, often fuelled by anti-Business political idealogy, of the vital link between Businesses locating in your area, being successful, training and employing people and paying Business rates.

## Be Fair – and Create the Right Environment for Business in Our Society

Socially inclusive wealth creation matters but, undeniably, there is a politically motivated anti-Business agenda. It may be well-intentioned, but the point is that it fails to appreciate how Business works and fails to acknowledge one of the most powerful forces regulating Business – the market. For example, the British Labour Party under Shadow Chancellor of the Exchequer John McDonnell would like to choose not only what industries thrive and how, but also whether their output is worthwhile or not. The financial sector, he stated, would be subject to a "new deal" requiring that its services deliver "a clear benefit to the whole community".

Fine words that sound good on the platform; who wouldn't vote for that? But then most people would vote for motherhood and apple pie as well. The problem is that the people who would decide whether or not it had passed this bar would be distant politicians. It seems to me that socialism wants to make everything either forbidden or compulsory – why? My concern is that actions like this remove the need for personal responsibility.

So, what needs to happen? Politicians need to encourage people to take risks and invest. They should make speeches and explain in their manifesto what they will do to make the entrepreneur or small Business person feel that they are on their side. We need the people that make the rules to be on the side of Business. And the politicians need it too.

Crucially, what socialism doesn't understand is that we live in a competitive world: partly because *Businesses* compete (for example, for investment, people, resources), and partly because *people* compete, that's always been our instinct and nature. As a society we compete for investment, and you will not attract an investor to your country because the weather is good, they'll come because it is worth their while. So we need low tax, and big signs encouraging people to come here.

## The John Lewis Partnership

Certainly not a model for every Business everywhere, but the philosophy behind and delivery of the model of the John Lewis Partnership provides a great deal of food for thought and can certainly help in the development of our thinking of how we can Fix Business.

The concept of the John Lewis Partnership (JLP) was created by John Spedan Lewis who, in 1929, during the rehabilitation process following a riding accident, came up with the partnership model which still endures today At the time he said it was "an experiment in industrial democracy" – these are the same words used regularly in the Business today. Why has it been so successful?

Andy Street, the CEO between 2007 and 2016, says the same seven founding principles are ruthlessly adhered to representing the Business today. He believes that the secret to ongoing success for the Business and its partners lies in continuous innovation and encouragement to be the best in class. He says the model itself is not enough to carry them through to the future. They must be brilliantly competitive and stay ahead of the game.

In a period of recession in 2008 JLP boldly embraced the challenge for online retailing and invested heavily, from retained profits, to be the epitome of a successful retail brand serving its customers, suppliers and partners in an entirely new marketplace. They were the first to offer "click and collect" at a time when others were very sceptical. How was this achieved? Mr Street believes there are two important reasons:

1. He was able to let the profit take the strain and was able to invest for the long term.

2. Everyone on board with the vision for the future rather than focusing on the past.

In the JLP model making decisions is not difficult. Despite the fact that all partners ("employees") have a stake in the Business, a management board is carefully selected to implement decisions whilst at the same time working closely with all "stakeholders". This was tested during Street's tenure when online activity created a surplus of staff to the tune of around 7,000 and all were made redundant. No one heard about that in the media, did they? Why? Because this was communicated across the Business working with partners to ensure the outcome was achieved in a positive and "humane" way. Indeed, JLP HR policies are robust and must always reflect the seven founding principles. It is proudly a Business that gives each partner a six-month sabbatical after 25 years and a final-salary, non-contributory pension, to the envy of many. How do they still make profits? Note to public sector.

When Mr Street took over the helm during the financial crash, he was heard to say "Don't waste a good crisis", believing he could spot an opportunity in developing the Business further when everyone else was re-trenching. How right he was. Another favourite saying of his is: "Paranoid on the upswing", meaning that you never take your eye off the ball. Even when everything is going well, you continuously strive to do things better.

He believes the continued success of JLP lies in the spirit of the community through its partners, suppliers, customers and the towns and cities in which they operate. All make a valuable contribution to the success of the Business. This has created a unique brand which is the envy of the retail world.

Why has no one else ever achieved the same level of success as JLP? Mr Street says that many think it's a utopian ideology when really it's like any other Business that has to make hard-nosed investment decisions. Many fall short of the "package" and go only part of the way in implementing the structure required. There has to be full commitment and diligent adherence to "the rules" or else it won't work. Everyone has to buy into the project and that will only be achieved by accepted confidence that "we are all in this together". It is not a model for every sector. But so many more Businesses and their employees (not to mention the reputation of Business and the cause of "taking everyone with you" in wealth creation) could benefit from such a modus operandi; it is to be hoped that many more Businesses seek to "make a difference" in this way.

## Finally, Do the Right Thing and Show Leadership

When I started at the CBI I began using the concept of socially inclusive wealth creation and organised lunches with executives from Businesses of different sizes. The purpose of these lunches was to convey my thinking and get people engaged with the key issues and challenges facing Business. During one such lunch, when I was explaining my ideas on socially inclusive wealth creation, an executive from a major UK bank interrupted and made the point that her priority was making as much money as possible for the shareholders of the bank (and they can then do whatever they want with their money). Not CSR. Not social inclusion. If it doesn't make money for the shareholders she's not interested.

Here's why she was wrong and what she was overlooking: if you operate in sympathy with the local community, by which I mean those people affected by your activities and operations, and if you understand and meet the need for wealth creation to be socially inclusive, then you will not only make money for your shareholders but it will be sustainable, durable and potentially longer-lasting. Her reply was that she didn't have that long to wait. I thought of her during the banking crisis and subsequently, when banks really could have done with more understanding, support and goodwill, especially in the court of public opinion.

What Business leaders need to accept is their leadership role, which includes the duty to do the right thing. Also important is the ability to acknowledge the insecurity that drives you on, but not to let that dominate your life. Every so often stop, smell the coffee and reappraise what you want to achieve in your life, what you have achieved and what you are achieving. Often, during a career, it will be the case that there are new challenges and opportunities needing new skills or a new approach. Is your Business tooled up with enough good people? Are they the right people to help the Business achieve? Are you doing enough, not only to skill and train the people who work in your Business, but also using the power of education and training in the wider community as the most tremendous agent for social inclusion that your wealth creation can deliver?

This is the challenge that I address in the next chapter: the value of education and training and the need to develop new skills if we are to continue Fixing Business.

## Key Questions

- What actions are you taking as a Business to support the communities in which you operate? How are these activities being viewed and what more can you do?
- Are you working actively with both sides of your supply chain to build more support in the local community? Are you getting politicians and media involved?
- Are you actively supporting Business? If not, why?
- What does "doing the right thing" mean to your employees and customers, and are you doing it – always?

- Are you involving everyone in your Business in your social inclusion initiatives? Whether it be in the area of skilling, training, the environment or community involvement, are you encouraging ideas from all of your employees, not just telling them what to do? Do you match time they give up with time you pay them for?
- Social inclusion benefits from recognition and widespread acceptance, so are you celebrating the work you do and encouraging others to provide support?

# CHAPTER 4

# HARNESSING THE POWER OF EDUCATION, TRAINING AND SKILLS

*"We all acknowledge the urgent need for major investment. We are all obsessed with investment in our physical infrastructure. Of course enhanced productivity and international competitiveness require this, but sustained investment in our human infrastructure is even more vital to deliver a socially cohesive, wealth-creative, productivity-enhancing, globally competitive UK."*

—Lord Digby Jones

## WHY IS EDUCATION, TRAINING AND SKILLS SUCH A VITAL BUSINESS ISSUE?

Increasing and improving education, training and skills (ETS) is a huge and ongoing challenge for our societies, and one where Business is both a customer, receiving and benefiting from education and training, and a supplier that is developing and supplying those skills. When it comes to fixing the reputation and standing of Business there is much more to be done in the areas of education, training and skills: specifically, there is more that Business needs, and more that Business can do to help.

Improving ETS is a big challenge for many complicated reasons but in large part because they are so vitally important at every level, affecting issues ranging from individual happiness and success through to Business's effectiveness and, finally, society's prosperity and the choices and decisions we all make collectively.

Crucially, education, training and skills are not issues that can ever be "settled". In part this is because they are so closely connected with other constantly shifting global issues such as demography, migration, technology and globalisation, which all affect the availability, accessibility and effectiveness of people. Above all, however, the context and need for ETS is dynamic: it changes and progresses with our situation and aspirations. It is probably not fully appreciated that there is a direct correlation between the free market Business imperative to develop and deliver products and services for customers, and the fact that doing this requires Business to hit a moving target; customers' aspirations, needs and expectations change, and new markets open up while others mature. All of this means that the needs of Business are never static and the quantity and nature of the skills they need to succeed is always changing. Clearly, that is one of the reasons why Business is such a stimulating and progressive area in which to work, but it does require flexibility and relevance in the way we manage our education systems. Too often, however, these qualities of flexibility and progressiveness, best described as a learning mindset, are sadly lacking.

ETS is so significant for Business. What follows in this chapter shines a light on the diverse range of issues at play. Hopefully our thinking about the future will be more broadly informed.

## THE FUTURE: A CHANGING JOBS' MARKET

It is essential to develop a flexible approach; one that favours openness and a desire for lifelong learning. Also there are skills that Business needs to strengthen, notably negotiating and cross-cultural working. Business skills need to keep developing and improving if Business is to stay competitive, and education needs constantly to reflect Business's changing priorities. Finally, education, training and skills are lifelong activities, not just for the young; they are valuable for everyone including (and especially) older people.

**Education, training and skills are lifelong activities, not just for the young; they are valuable for everyone including (and especially) older people.** Indeed, Business has a vital role through ETS in helping to deal with what I think is the most pressing threat to the developed world's economic survival over the next hundred years: an ageing population. There was never enough money to pay pensions, it's just that no-one lived long enough to find that out! We kid ourselves if we think that increased taxation will pay for the health and social care required by millions of older people in the decades ahead. Socialists believe that getting Facebook to pay "their fair share of tax" (whatever that may mean) will somehow pay for the social and healthcare consequences of us all living longer.

One area in which something can be done, and quickly, is increased and better use of those in "the new sixties"; that is, those in their seventies. The needs of the job market have changed, working from home is technologically easy, money is not always such an imperative in the job choice for an older person and employers tend to get a more loyal employee: but older employees will need confidence-boosting training and constant upskilling and a feeling of being included … just like everyone else. The economy will benefit, the call on pensions (and possibly healthcare) will be less and even the Exchequer will swell a tad.

## What We Know for Certain about the Jobs of the Future: They Will be Very Different

In the future there will be an unprecedented number of jobs that simply don't exist today. It has of course always been thus. Global, societal, market, community, public sector needs and innovative solutions initially outstrip people's skills base, their willingness to change and their ability to cope through upskilling and reskilling with such change.

We see this simple truth reshaping work and Business already, largely driven by the rise of technology in general and digitalisation in particular, and the trend shows no sign of slowing. Highlighting this point are those jobs that did not exist at the turn of the century:

- **Social Media Manager.** With over three-quarters of adults that are online participating in social media in some form, there has been a sudden and dramatic rise in jobs such as "Social Media Manager", whose sole responsibility is the management of a company's social networks. The importance and colossal potential of social media, not only for creating opportunities and connecting with customers but also managing risk and engaging key constituents, has only been recognised in the last few years. There is no point in having experts, great products and good values if the team cannot use "of-the-moment" routes to market; gaps in the knowledge of proper and productive use of social media for everyone from the sales assistant to the CEO must be plugged … and quickly. What must be avoided is the possibility that social media loses its way and becomes as reviled as, say, tobacco because its social deficiencies are seen to outweigh its economic and relationship advantages.

- **Digital Marketing Specialist.** As late as 2005 most marketing was still offline. There was email and websites but social media marketing, search marketing and all the other strands of digital marketing were still in their infancy. Now, in the second decade of the 21st century, marketing has completely changed so that Businesses with the right people and skills are now able to connect better with more people and in a more personal, targeted, cost-effective and relevant way than ever before. On Black Friday 2016, for the first time, the John Lewis Partnership sold more products on their website than in their stores; the marketing landscape has changed forever.

- **SEO Specialist.** Search engine optimisation is one of the most valuable digital jobs and one which, as little as five years ago, was still in its infancy. Now, if people and Businesses want to be discovered online and found via search engines such as Google, then SEO optimisation is the answer. An SEO specialist helps a Business to upgrade their website so that it appears on the first page of search results, as well as improving the searchability of content so that it regularly features in keyword searches.

- **App Designer and Developer.** The Apple App Store and Android stores have been in existence for less than 10 years, but their arrival has brought many new jobs into the digital economy. Mobile apps are more and more common, and whereas smartphone users were once grateful and impressed, they now simply expect them to be available, relevant and impressive. App Designers produce the graphics and functionality for new apps and app updates, and App Developers implement the design and put it into code, making sure that the app works as it is supposed to, without any problems.

- **Cloud Services Manager.** No, not a rainmaker: a Cloud Services Manager is something altogether different. This area of expertise includes anyone that is an expert in the mechanisms, devices, technologies and usage of Cloud storage technologies and services. Cloud storage of data is another area that has grown exponentially, and as it has grown other aspects of the job have emerged as well including, for example, online security which has developed into a sector all of its own, requiring new skills and practised application.

- **Blogger.** The term, which originated as "web logger", has been around since the late 1990s when blogs originally started as online diaries. However they soon grew in popularity in the early 2000s, gaining a much wider readership. As recently as a few years ago blogs such as the Huffington Post, Techcrunch, The Drudge Report and LifeHacker were largely unheard of, but now blogging is a valuable skill and the industry is making millions and completely knocking more established Businesses, such as print media, back on their heels.

Not only are there many, many more different types of job today than we imagined only a decade ago, but the nature of work and

> **"The one thing computers have done is let us make bigger mistakes. We have to be careful not to depend on our machines."**
>
> **Michael Bloomberg**

the job market is much more fluid and dynamic than ever. New jobs emerge, and they can fade away just as quickly. Secretaries, typists, booksellers, travel agents, photograph developers, fax and telex service engineers are all occupations in which large numbers of skilled people were employed in the memory of people that are still working. Now they are either jobs of the past or, at best, peripheral, exceptional roles that are becoming ever more scarce and specialist. It is not just that new jobs are being created but also that old ones are changing out of all recognition or disappearing altogether. The rate of change is exponential; while there are those who remember the world of the wireless, warming your hands on the pipes at school and thinking a Big Mac was your older sister's raincoat, there are Millennials at work today who were not even born when the fax machine was indispensable!

## The Need: Business as a Customer for Education and Training

When I ask bosses what is the greatest problem they face in their Business, regardless of its size, location or sector, the answer is always the same: "Can't get enough skilled people." Despite low unemployment in the UK, a perceived lack of talent continues to keep many CEOs awake at night. This anxiety is not simply about not having enough supply of labour: it's about not having the right mix of capabilities. These are the skills needed to be competitive, to innovate and to build a sustainable Business. The problem is the speed at which these capabilities are needed and the rate at which they change.

Consider the curriculum in universities today. The research, validation, design, teaching and assessment timeline can take several years to complete. This means that it is not unusual for the class of 2017 to have been taught examples from the turn of the century which are now probably out of date in terms of relevance. We are teaching our children skills for a different age, a situation that has been described by UNICEF's Global Head of Education as "static knowledge". So, despite the unprecedented numbers of people achieving degrees and A grades, this historical time lag plays out across the education system. This situation also combines with worrying increases in social exclusion, with many young people falling behind and opting out.

These problems are evident not just in what we teach but also how we teach. Our schools and colleges are already struggling with a generational learning gap, so how do we ensure that today's digital natives make sense of the cold formality of classrooms and lecture halls? There is a crisis of relevance, not only in educational subject matter but also with the educators themselves.

The fundamental problem with our education systems is that they were invented in the 19th century to provide a workforce for an industrial age. Despite being created over a century ago many of the beliefs and practices remain: the "teacher as expert" at the front of the class, the age-based cohorts, the line-ups and bells. The tragedy is that we are not living in a golden age; we are living in a world where we face some of our biggest challenges, and we are failing employers with an insufficient and irrelevant skills mix. Worse than that, however, we are also failing our children just at a time when we need them to be the most versatile and resilient generation in history.

## The Solution: Business as Supplier of Education and Training

So, given that the future is so dynamic, with jobs that don't even exist today and changing pressures and priorities for Business, what is the solution? The answers lie with Business being a much more effective provider of education, training and skills, rather than being a passive consumer. There are many ways that this can happen but three are particularly significant: apprenticeships, academies, and lifelong learning.

## VISION OF THE FUTURE #1: MORE AND BETTER APPRENTICESHIPS

There is a fond remembrance in the UK for apprenticeships, and little wonder. In the 1950s and 1960s they provided young people with relevant skills that led to a lifetime of employment. They also satisfied a need among many young people for practical skills rather than academic or theoretical ones. Clearly there is a valuable place for the study of subjects such as politics, philosophy and economics, but this should not be at the expense of technical or practical skills such as mechanical and electrical engineering and construction, or vocational skills such as nursing and teaching. We need to encourage more and more apprenticeships of every type: those that address current and future Business needs, such as the need for App Designers and Digital Marketers; those that address service roles, such as tourism, hospitality and financial services; and those that are perennially important roles, notably apprenticeships relating to engineering, construction and manufacturing. It is in the best interests of Business to design and deliver these apprenticeships so that they generate a steady supply of the most relevant, capable and skilled employees.

Many companies in the UK do all this very well. Indeed there are very few large Businesses – so deeply immersed in the global search and race for talent that "grow your own" is a sine qua non – who don't have first-class apprenticeship schemes; but they could do so much more to "force" (or maybe the euphemism "partner with" would be a better phrase) their supply base in all areas and of all sizes to do the same.

## VISION OF THE FUTURE #2: ACADEMIES

A particularly inspiring and exciting vision of the future is provided by the growth of academies. British Prime Minister Tony

One of the most frequent arguments used against investing in training and professional development is "What happens if I train my people and they leave?" Surely a much better question is "What happens if I don't train them and they stay?"

Blair introduced privately sponsored academies as a way of targeting deprived areas with the aim primarily of making engineering, manufacturing and other practical and more vocational subjects both inspirational and aspirational. Their growth has been relatively slow (and facing ideologically inspired political obstruction at various levels hasn't helped) but their potential to make a positive, relevant and lasting impact on education and training remains considerable.

One impressive example of what Business-supported academies can achieve is provided by engineering firm JCB. As well as taking apprentices to work in their Business, JCB have also established an academy housed in the inspiring setting of Arkwright's mill, one of the crucibles of the industrial revolution, where young students of secondary school age are taught practical skills. The "offer" from JCB's academy is that if you go to the school, and work hard and diligently, then you will be guaranteed a job. Crucially the school curriculum is based on realistic challenges set by employers. The school's results in maths and English are excellent, and while there is acknowledgement of the value of the humanities these take a back seat at JCB's academy. Instead, there is a clear focus on learning by doing, with attributes of perseverance and determination emphasised.

The relatively slow growth of academies highlights one important challenge: most of the people deciding the nature of our education system – for example, civil servants working in the UK Department for Education – are academics; individuals who are likely to look unfavourably on practical work whose many merits include a direct relevance for Business. This attitude needs to change: it not only harms Business, it also does a disservice to the many young people who find a career in this area to be fulfilling, productive and worthwhile. Academies are actively encouraging many more girls and young women to enter professions such as engineering, while many dyslexics find this practical environment one in which they can thrive. Policymakers need to review curricula to ensure their relevance; they need to value outcomes and results, not simply inputs; they need to ensure that children are skilled for the jobs of tomorrow (most graduates are simply not ready for work) and they need to strive to produce an education that meets the needs of the country – not simply follow a path that is now decades old.

Between 35 and 40% of people won't pay back their student loan, so why go to a non-Russell group university in the UK and pile up debt when you could be paid for your degree and work at the same time? The education system is out of line with the needs of Business, and the adult training and skills sector also needs to be adjusted to meet its needs. Leave school, embark on an apprenticeship (maybe at sixteen or maybe at eighteen) in any one of a multitude of subjects and then go to university later on and your employer will pay for it and pay you at the same time! The employer gets a more relevantly trained employee and the employee becomes instantly more employable – at no cost and no student loan! Finally, small Businesses need to take the initiative themselves and make it happen: actively develop or find the skills you need. Don't sit by and wait for the ideal employee to walk through the door; get to work shaping that individual now.

Surely the sheer importance of education to our nation's ability to win through in this, the most brutally competitive of centuries, calls for the depoliticisation of education; leave ideological baggage at the door. A word here perhaps about that other contentious educational "innovation": the grammar school. The government's new controversial policy that local authorities and communities may create new grammar schools has never dictated that they *must* come into being; they are merely giving people choice. What on earth is wrong with giving a bright kid from a challenged home a route out of straitened circumstances into the improved world of better life choices that a testing, challenging education can provide? Socialist ideology dictates that everyone should be dumbed down to the lowest common denominator. What is the result? By abolishing or campaigning against selection by ability they have ended up with something worse: selection by ability to afford it. Faced with a poor state school, parents who can do so pay for their children's education at better schools (don't they Diane

Abbott?!) or buy a (more expensive) house in the catchment area of a good state school.

## VISION OF THE FUTURE #3: LIFELONG LEARNING THAT HAS RELEVANCE

When discussing education much of the focus is, quite rightly, on children and young people. There is a natural tension between a range of objectives that are not always complementary, for example: ensuring basic literacy and numeracy and providing the essentials across different subjects; opening up young minds to a world of possible careers, vocations and opportunities; teaching life skills (such as leadership and teamworking); developing Business skills and, increasingly, helping people adjust to a world of ambiguity and change, where yesterday's certainties are being replaced with new and unfamiliar situations, risks and opportunities.

> Learning works best when it has context and relevance. This is one of the many benefits of modern Business-focused academies.

In these circumstances, there is a need to recognise that information, knowledge and data are now an indispensable part of the modern world; what matters is the ability to make sense of the data, finding patterns and trends, and sharing information with the right people at the right time.

Also, the world of Business in the 21st century is one beset with change, volatility and crises. As a result, a mindset that emphasises openness, humility, a desire to learn and a willingness to take action when needed is vital, as it provides the best defence for today's leaders against challenges which are increasingly complex, volatile and unexpected. It will be a case of not what we know that matters, but how we react to what we don't know. Of course, being confidently receptive to what we don't know and not bigoted or closed in our minds is an essential ingredient to successful exploitation of lifelong learning.

The certainties of the past are being challenged and dismantled; the challenge we now all face is unlearning what we thought we knew, and changing our minds to take account of drastically different and evolving realities and circumstances. This highlights another crucial point about education, training and skills: the need for managers and leaders within Business to step up personally and constantly to take responsibility for the "how" as well as the "what".

## What Business Leaders Can Do to Develop Skills, Effectiveness and Performance

There are several things you can do with your team to develop performance. These can be completed at any time, and crucially they should not simply wait to be part of an appraisal process:

- **Actively manage your team's performance.** Prepare a presentation explaining the most significant issues and priorities for your team. Discuss the impact of this – for example, how it affects workload and responsibilities, any potential challenges and how these may be overcome.

- **Establish 'support and challenge' groups of four or five people.** Each group meets informally, either weekly or monthly, with each member spending 10 minutes explaining, uninterrupted, about a challenge or issue they face. The other members of the group then ask questions and provide comments to help their colleague to progress or solve the issue.

## Age Sensitive Management

### Managing Across Generations

Different age groups in the workforce have different needs – and this is especially the case when it comes to education and training, two issues that undeniably affect overall corporate performance and morale.

An increasing number of organisations, including Tesco, the UK's largest retailer, employ people of different age groups so that their workforce is more representative of society as a whole. This enables them to relate well to their customers who are, of course, a wide range of ages. This approach also requires a new and tailored focus on training, so that the skills that are needed are consistently available for the entire workforce.

Any contemporary workplace should contain four age groups:

- Silent veterans: Born 1945 and before
- Baby boomers: Born 1946 to 1964
- Generation X: Born 1965 to 1981
- Millennials: Born 1982 onwards.

Age-sensitive management suggests that these different groups have different expectations, experiences and training needs, and therefore require different styles of management and different approaches.

For example:

**Silent veterans** tend to have the most traditional ideas of interaction, favouring formal contact and face-to-face meetings. They typically value recognition of their skills and abilities, for example with awards and ceremonies.

When managing **baby boomers**, clearly define goals and break down the process into a series of individual targets. Place an emphasis on teamwork and motivational talks. Rewards should be public and noticeable displays of recognition.

Allow **Generation X** slightly more freedom to achieve their targets: tell them what to do, but allow them to decide how to achieve the goal. Keep channels of communication open to allow ideas, opinions and feedback to be discussed in a candid and honest way. Practical rewards, such as days off or monetary bonuses, are welcomed.

**Millennials** should be given plenty of opportunities to build their skills and experience – view yourself partially as a teacher as well as a boss. Find out their personal goals and make broader company targets relevant to those individual goals. Communication should be informal and positive. Given that this is the group that will be the future of the workplace in years to come, we need to develop flexibility and openness in them from the outset.

---

Training and developing ranked higher than cash bonuses for some Millennials. Millennials not only seek continuous improvement and development, but also expect their employers to provide them with the opportunities.

According to a recent study by Instructure, creators of the modern learning and training platform Bridge, 54% of managers feel millennials are only somewhat prepared to contribute to a company right from when they start. On the other hand, millennials are eager to learn and engage. More than 20% of this generation feel their employer-provided technologies are pretty terrible. Thankfully, this "largest generation" happen to be very ambitious, but only if the training is on its terms.

---

- **Review the budget or operating plan and assess progress** each quarter. Highlight and assign priority actions, monitor progress and provide support.

- **Produce a list of major challenges** facing the Business and, together with your colleagues, decide how to resolve them.
- **Encourage team members to plan.** You can ask an individual to specify exactly what needs to be achieved by checking for holes in their logic or any ambiguities in their plan. Also, check that the plan is achievable with the skills available and discuss realistic milestones.
- **Record things that worked well.** This helps you to identify those activities that are most effective and eliminate those that aren't. Consider offering assistance – this will strengthen the team either by the sharing of expertise or by reducing the load. Finally, set new goals as this will help move you forward in both Business and personal terms.
- **Set challenging, audacious and relevant goals.** Goals are valuable for focusing activity and achieving success. It is important, when goal-setting, to be clear about the big picture – the vision and Business priorities.
- **"Walk the talk".** Give team members an example of the approach you value and find out where each team member needs help or support. You may not be able to solve a problem yourself but you should be able to help them find their own solutions.
- **Convey a sense of urgency and enthusiasm.** Five prominent personal qualities of successful leaders are self-confidence, energy, empathy, conviction and vision. When conveying a sense of urgency and enthusiasm, it can help to measure

yourself against these qualities (or, if you prefer, decide which qualities are most significant and then assess how you could improve in these areas). If any one of these qualities is weak or missing then your effectiveness will be diminished. Also important is the fact that each factor affects the others. So, for example, weak skills in one area (e.g. empathy) lead to weakness in others (e.g. communicating). These five qualities are closely related and drive each other.

- **Use a 360-degree appraisal.** Open, constructive feedback is invaluable. A 360-degree appraisal provides insights from subordinates, peers and bosses and can draw attention to areas of improvement as well as providing a different perspective.

- **Confront poor performance.** When an employee's performance falls short of the goals and objectives that were mutually established you must address the situation. Here are some guidelines to help:
  - Act earlier rather than later, to avoid letting the issue grow.
  - Collect evidence to support your case, explore the reasons for poor performance and give specific and balanced feedback.
  - Focus on employee behaviour rather than attitude or personality.
  - Discuss the facts about actual performance and compare with what is desired.
  - Always praise in public; also criticise, but in private.
  - Never embarrass the person.

- Make certain that the employee agrees that there is a gap in performance, discuss possible reasons for the gap and agree a plan of action to close it.
- Provide support as the employee works to improve. For example, offer coaching.
- Ensure that everyone knows that whilst a great deal of coaching and training will be offered, in the end square pegs just will not go into round holes: difficult decisions have to be taken and sympathetically, generously but firmly implemented. It is fair to the person (they nearly always know they have no future) and everyone else expects it, so morale goes up not down when firm but fair leadership is displayed. Not tolerating (and being seen not to tolerate) second best is expected and a worthy aspiration of leadership.
- Give frequent feedback on progress.
- Acknowledge when the desired level has been achieved and sustained.
- **Choose the best methods of training and development for team members.** One of the biggest dangers a leader can face is to assume that there are only a few methods for learning; there are many, and some of the most popular are listed below. Choosing the type of development that is most appropriate often depends on: cost, time available for development, the type of individual and their particular learning style, the immediate needs of the task and of the job role, and the long-term needs of that role.

| Type of activity | Benefits | Disadvantages |
|---|---|---|
| External short courses (normally between one and five days) | Intensive expert tuition | Expensive<br>Can be difficult to relate to the work environment<br>Duration and timing |
| In-house training | Tailored | Expensive<br>Potential personality clashes<br>Trainees' reluctance |
| Job shadowing | Relevant and work-based<br>Low cost | Picking up bad practices<br>Does not generate innovation |
| Distance learning | Learning at a pace and place that is most convenient | Requires self-discipline<br>Can feel isolating |
| Qualification programmes (e.g. certificates, diplomas, degrees) | Thorough and rigorous<br>Meet specified, recognised standards<br>Encourages the individual | Time-consuming<br>Expensive<br>Not necessarily relevant or practical |
| Reading | Inexpensive<br>Tailored | No feedback |
| Software packages | Consistent method<br>Can be interactive<br>Useful for technical skills | Expensive<br>Frustrating if there is no feedback |
| Research projects | Self-directed<br>Work-based | Need self-discipline<br>Need specific research skills |
| Outward bound courses | Team-building<br>Confidence-building | Can be uncomfortable<br>Expensive<br>May lack job relevance |
| Role playing | Inexpensive<br>Focused<br>Shared experiences | Can be uncomfortable<br>Success largely depends on the quality of feedback |

(*continued*)

| Type of activity | Benefits | Disadvantages |
|---|---|---|
| Workshops | Can mix internal perspectives with external views | Can be easily dominated by others |
| Learning from other people's experience | Good learning opportunities across a broad range | Can be subjective and broad |
| Day release/ evening classes | Interaction with others Clear focus on the topic | Expensive Timing can cause problems |
| Team training | Character building Competitive Relatively economical | Deters those with less self-confidence |
| Lecture method | Relatively economical Focused | Academic textbook delivery |
| Business games | Engaging Team building | Deter those with less self-confidence |
| Coaching and mentoring | Focused Suits individuals | Emphasis on coach/ mentor's own opinions and methods |

## But Business Needs Support

Business cannot accept this challenge alone.

The public sector is a huge employer in the UK. Democratic capitalism around the world will now and forever expect more and better public services and to pay less for them. The only successful way to achieve this is reform; reform of delivery mechanisms, reform of how taxpayers' investment is used, reform of expectation, reform of obligation. Equipping the public-sector employee (wherever he is or whatever she does) with the skills and thus the confidence to understand and deal with change, with better use of kit, with flexibility in the how, the where and the when, is so incredibly important: to our country, to our individual needs and to our pockets. Business (as the generator of the taxes that pay for the public sector) has every right to expect the other half of the economy to espouse the 21st century Education Training & Skills agenda in just the same way.

And as for Business having one hand tied behind its back, every employer in the country, whether in the public or private sector, has the right to expect that, after 11 years of full-time, free, compulsory education every child leaves school being able to read, write, count and operate a computer. The ETS agenda will only work if the raw material coming out of our schools has the necessary basic education and is thus fit for the enormously competitive 21st-century world of work. Being forced to build our "skilled house" on foundations of sand is a disgrace; governments, of whatever political stripe, should take action against teachers and parents who let down themselves, the taxpayer, their country and most importantly the children by failing in this basic duty. And failing they are: nearly half the young people in the UK leave school at sixteen being unable to read, write or count to the standard expected of an 11-year-old. Little wonder that just under 20% of the adult population cannot read to the standard we would expect of a child leaving primary school!

Teachers should have contractual responsibility to ensure that pupils can achieve basic literacy, numeracy and computer skills by the age of 12, medical condition absent. Their justifiable complaint that they receive little or no support from some parents should be accommodated by such parents being denied an element of their welfare benefits until their children, medical condition absent, achieve the basic level of skills. Surely the taxpayer and the future employer are entitled to better, much better, from the nation's education system and from some parents who clearly fail to accept even such a low level of responsibility.

If education is about how to develop, nurture and harness the most important natural resource available to Business — its people – then the next chapter looks at how to value and protect every other natural resource. Issues of sustainability and environmental protection matter to everyone in society, including Business, and as with education, Business has a role to play both as a beneficiary of environmental protection and as an actor.

In Fixing Business, in winning back public appreciation, in winning the perception war, there can be no bigger gun in the armoury than being seen to play a major part in arming the next generation for a world of work that is frightening and ever-changing, yet that will hold no fears for those of any age in any sector or any part of the country who are tooled up ready for the fight:

Bring it on!

**If you think training's expensive, try ignorance.**

## Key Questions

- Does your Business offer apprenticeships and practical opportunities for young people?
- What more could you do to help develop the skills of the future? What skills do you have in your organisation and what do you need? What different skills and at what level will you need in three years' time?
- What is the best way to develop your people?
- How connected are you with local schools and colleges? Do you support their work and actively share with them a Business agenda? Do you give a local teacher or lecturer a week's experience in your Business with a properly structured programme?
- Do you actively employ older people? Do you provide cross-generational performance management?
- What more could you do in your Business to develop skills and performance in your Business or team?

# CHAPTER 5

# PROTECTING THE ENVIRONMENT: AN ESSENTIAL PRIORITY

*"Earth provides enough to satisfy every man's needs, but not every man's greed."*

—Mahatma Gandhi

When I started to promote my vision of socially inclusive wealth creation in my early days as Director-General of the CBI, I would always state in speeches how one of the three pillars of my vision was how Business and its wealth-creative process had "to be sensitive, and be seen to be sensitive, to Planet Earth, for this is the only home we've all got".

Many found these words at odds with some of my other statements in my lobbying efforts. I did not, but I could see the cause for their confusion. I never bought into how climate change was entirely man-made, but neither did I believe that man had nothing to do with the obvious changes to the climates around the world. Climate change is a natural phenomenon but mankind's ignorant, selfish acts against the natural world only accelerate the pace of change and make a worrying situation so much worse.

But I found (and still do) the "thought police" and politically correct attitudes of many of the Green lobby so wrong. Even the BBC were at it now and again and were sometimes hauled over the coals for biased reporting. People were condemned, vilified, for holding views that were at odds with the Green mainstream. And when it was revealed that some climate change zealots had fiddled the data to suit their prejudice, I felt that my instincts were justified. You could be forgiven for reaching the conclusion that caring for the planet was all wrapped up in a socialist, anti-Business, anti-capitalist agenda.

The true motivations of organisations such as Friends of the Earth are open to suspicion, following the news in early January 2017 that the charity had been ordered by the Advertising Standards Authority to withdraw leaflets about the impact of fracking for shale gas because allegations contained in them could not be supported with evidence. The fundraising leaflet said that fracking increased the risk of cancer and asthma for local residents and would cause water contamination, plummeting house prices and higher insurance bills. "A toxic cocktail of chemicals" used in fracking "could end up in your drinking water", causing problems with eyes, skin and the nervous system, according to Friends of the Earth. The leaflet was illustrated with a picture of Grasmere in the Lake District National Park, where there are no plans for fracking. I have been left querying the veracity and values of an organisation that so often accuses Business of falsifying the facts.

I was rightly quoted as criticising the Blair government for being prepared to sacrifice our country's global competitiveness "on the altar of green credentials".

I was hugely critical (and still am) of Prime Minister Blair for committing the UK to such a reduction in greenhouse gas emissions in such a short time, merely to reach the moral high ground at an EU Summit, that the ability of UK Business to compete with our EU rivals would be severely impaired.

I failed to understand why the Brown government insisted on its ministers being driven round in hybrid cars made in Japan when their wages were paid out of tax generated in part by the production of marvellous cars in Britain, often by welcomed manufacturers headquartered in Japan but doing their stuff in our country.

I saw the ill-conceived Climate Change Levy of 2002 as the sheer waste of hard-earned money it surely was. On this I was in rare but significant agreement with the TUC!

I shouted from every rooftop the cause of nuclear-generated energy, warning that our old fleet of nuclear power stations would be decommissioned and that the successive Green Papers, White Papers, policy workshops, keynote speeches and lobby briefings of the Blair government were silent on the nuclear issue. Nothing, absolutely nothing, was done for years, for fear, in 2003, of upsetting the left-wing Green lobby – how a government with a thumping great majority and an opposition in disarray can be politically frightened is beyond me! I constantly warned that investment in nuclear energy was not an overnight decision and implementation of policy would take two decades. And still Nero fiddled. I even stated on the BBC Today Programme that a very cold winter in 2015–2020 would lead to the lights going out and no amount of building of windmills would sort out that problem. I was told I was being alarmist. Only massive reliance on fossil fuels has prevented this emergency; absolutely not what the Green lobby would want.

So we have today a Great Britain that is incapable of building nuclear power stations without the highly incentivised assistance of the French and the Chinese. So many of our universities don't teach or research nuclear physics because the subject was left to wither on the vine of indifference for decades as successive governments dithered. We, the country that gave the Free World its first nuclear power generator at Calder Hall, have become a nuclear eunuch at precisely the time the power generation/reduction in carbon emissions equation is being solved in part by nuclear power. There is so much that Business could do in this field, with investment, training, routes to market that would help the country and help Business be seen as a force for good ... if only it was allowed to!

Yet just because Her Majesty's Government was inept at implementation, just because I could never unravel the statements of the Green Party and Friends of the Earth on the environment from a wider socialist, Business-hating agenda, just because I could not see what on earth was environmentally friendly about George Monbiot stating on the day fox hunting was banned that this was "the last great act of the Class War" (and I don't even approve of fox hunting!) didn't mean that I did not wish Business to get its house in order on matters environmental nor that I didn't see so much good in a lot of the Green agenda.

## SAVE THE PLANET! ... BUT THE PLANET WILL BE FINE!

For years I have been saying in speeches that the people who say we must "do something or the Planet will die" are wrong. The Planet will be fine I say; it is we, mankind, who will die

**"What is the use of a house if you haven't got a tolerable planet to put it on?"**

**Henry David Thoreau**

out, become extinct. We've only been around, on the twenty-four hour clock of Earth's existence, for just a minute or so; our planet has withstood much greater onslaughts than that from pathetic Man. We will finally bring about our own destruction; become extinct, the Earth will have a geological enema for a few millennia and then one day a little creature will come out of the sea, sprout legs ... and off we'll go again!

Little did I know that, while I've been merrily addressing audiences the world over for many years with these words, way back in 1993 when I was still a journeyman lawyer in Birmingham, someone was pursuing a similar theme in writings that were read by millions. In researching for this book I came across what one of Michael Crichton's characters says in his novel *Jurassic Park*:

"You think man can destroy the Planet? What intoxicating vanity ... We've been residents here for the blink of an eye."

"If all the nuclear weapons in the World went off at once, if everything died ... Life would survive somewhere ... Earth has survived everything in its time ... sooner or later ... life would spread again."

"If we're gone tomorrow the Earth will not miss us."

## It's Good for Business … and it's Good Business

There are many different routes to take if Business is to be fixed. One of the essential tenets of socially inclusive wealth creation is for Business to be more environmentally sensitive as it goes about its wealth creation.

> **"Earth would survive our folly, only we would not."**
> **Michael Crichton**

Obviously this makes good Business sense; people like working for employers who show, by what they do and not just what they say, that they are respectful of the environment they affect by their actions and they make a positive contribution to a sustainable future for mankind's future on Earth. Consumers experience the feel-good factor in deciding to spend their hard-earned cash on goods or services from a provider who ticks the box for environmentally sensitive behaviour.

The very nature of creating wealth pollutes. Even the trader sitting in front of her screen creating tax-generating wealth in Wall Street or Canary Wharf pollutes.

The screen is powered by electricity which is generated by …
She came into work (Boris bike users excepted!) via a mode of polluting transport.
She works in a building of which cement constitutes a large component.
She will probably fly either for work or on holiday.

Two-thirds of all industrial methane and carbon dioxide released into the atmosphere since 1854 can be traced to burning fossil fuels and producing cement.

Business does not want to be the cause of so many illnesses caused by pollution, of course it doesn't. So everything it does, every little thing an individual Business achieves to lessen its contribution to the pollution issue, should be the subject of publicity, should be the subject of explanation to employees and customers alike, should be something to be proud of.

**"Water, water everywhere Nor any drop to drink."**

*The Rime of the Ancient Mariner* by Samuel Taylor Coleridge

Sea levels are rising. Whether caused by thermal expansion due to warming of the oceans or increased melting of land-based ice or both, it is an incontrovertible fact.

Forty percent of the population of the USA lives in relatively high-population-density coastal areas, where the sea level plays a role in flooding, shoreline erosion and storm hazards. If, as expected, the oceans rise between 2.5 and 6.5 feet by 2100 then many of the cities along the US Eastern Seaboard will be swamped. Globally, eight of the world's ten largest cities are near a coast, according to the United Nations' Atlas of the Oceans.

London, one of the top three Business capitals in the world, is vulnerable to flooding and especially exposed to the funnel effect of a coalescence of high tide, storm and rising sea level. Imagine the damage to Business if London "went under". And calculate the cost of sea defences and barriers to make sure it doesn't!

The Maldives is the world's lowest country and "could become the first state in history to be completely erased by the sea," according to Evan Puschak of The Seeker Network. On average, it's only five feet above current sea level; 77% of the Maldives will be underwater on current trends by 2100. Now the Maldives has quite a small population of around 350,000, but the "top six" countries most threatened by rising sea levels are China, India, Bangladesh, Vietnam, Indonesia and Japan. That's a handful of countries but with a total population of some three billion people! So many nations are justifiably concerned about potentially the greatest migration of peoples the world has ever seen; what happens when so many of the population in those six countries are forced to move? The social pressures, the racial tensions, the huge economic squeeze, the effects on food supplies, transport, clean water, healthcare … and the knock-on effect causing settled populations to up sticks and move ever westwards.

So this really matters to Business. It will affect markets, available labour, logistics, raw materials … and if Fixing Business is about doing the right thing (and being seen to do the right thing) because it's

**"Fixing Business is about doing the right thing because it's actually just the right thing to do."**

actually the right thing to do, can there be a better way of seeing the effects of doing nothing than watching people's very existence literally washed away?

## Business isn't the Problem; it's the Solution

**"Problems are not stop signs, they are guidelines."**

**Robert H. Schiller**

The Green lobby may think it's possible to live in a carbon-emission-free world but it isn't. People are indulging in a permanent bout of hypocrisy; they want to have their cake (a cuddly polar bear or the knowledge that an Asian peasant farmer's child has a roof over its head) and eat it (the unfettered freedom to switch on their electric light, drive their car, catch that flight or leave the tap running).

Moreover, the developing world is not calling a halt on massive, industrial, polluting expansion any time soon. China alone represents a 23.43% share of global $CO_2$ emissions! India (5.7%), Russia (4.87%) and Brazil (4.17%) are in the top five but together they only add up to just over half of China's share. But they are all on an unstoppable course of growing their economies. Indeed, when I was Minister of State for UK Trade and Investment, I shared a platform with several Indian cabinet ministers at a Business and trade summit in Bangalore. One of their very senior ministers looked at me during his speech and said in very polite but pointed tones: "My country has much catching up to do to achieve parity with your country; we are not going to inhibit our growth and slow down our progress by obeying a set of green rules that your country got rich by ignoring."

But there is one country in that top five (at number two, in fact) that can afford to, and frankly should, set a better example. The USA accounts for a 14.69% share of global $CO_2$ emissions. It has never entered into any binding treaty to curb greenhouse gases although, to be fair, it has nevertheless cut more carbon dioxide emissions than any other nation. But many "nice-to-haves" are now seen as essentials in the fight to get the economy back to pre-2008 levels, and as the new President's rhetoric definitely puts environmental issues at the bottom of the White House agenda, the chances of the USA losing its number two slot in the near future are slim.

So, if some countries refuse to add cost to what they do or make how they compete in a brutally competitive globalised economy more expensive, how can Business help and be seen to help? The European Union is relatively on the side of the angels on this one. The UK is a leader in Europe, but when so many other competing economies are not following the same path a lot of Business operations in the UK are rendered uncompetitive … and don't blame Business for that! The upside is that they have the moral high ground; the downside is that many operational bases have been priced out of the UK because of high energy costs (primarily due to green levies) and excessive regulation. Interestingly, politicians and those who vote for them want the green label but don't want the high electricity bills and job losses that come with it. "Principles cost" is definitely in the "do as I say, not as I do" category on this subject.

## Top causes for rising carbon emissions:

- **Burning coal, oil and gas.** This produces carbon dioxide and nitrous oxide.
- **Cutting down forests.** Trees help to regulate the climate by absorbing $CO_2$.
- **Increasing livestock farming.** Cows and sheep produce large amounts of methane when they digest their food.
- **Using fertilisers containing nitrogen.** This produces nitrous oxide emissions.
- **Using fluorinated gases.** This produces a very strong warming effect; up to 23,000 times greater than $CO_2$.

The real solution will be technologically-based. Technological advance will come from research and development promoted by governments and conducted by universities in tandem with Business. So many of the solutions can make money but willing purchasers are needed. Such willingness can be enforced by regulation, or by the alternative being too costly, or by developing economies being led in the right direction by cooperation at government level, or by operators finding that markets in, say, Europe are blocked to them because consumers are reluctant to buy from environmentally-insensitive manufacturers. But once again that requires the "do as I say, not as I do" brigade to have a change of heart.

## Ready for Take-Off

**Checking-in Passenger: "I'm checked to New York but I'd like that bag to go to Paris and that one to go to Sydney."**
**Check-in Clerk: 'I'm sorry Sir but that isn't possible."**
**Checking-in Passenger: "I don't know why it isn't. You did it last week and I didn't even have to ask!"**

The progress the automobile sector has made, and continues to make, in cutting emissions has been amazing. Use of lightweight construction materials, engine cut-offs and, above all else, the development of hybrid and electric cars. But for some truly impressive examples of how technology has made an enormous difference in the fight to keep mankind on this planet we should look at the aerospace sector.

Improved efficiency of an aircraft leads to less fuel being consumed, which leads to lower carbon dioxide emissions and reduced operating costs – a clear example of where good environmental sense means good Business sense as well.

Aerodynamics and engine performance are the largest contributors to increased efficiency, but reducing the weight of the aircraft is also vital and major advances, driven by the Business imperative, have been made technologically. The *Financial Times* helpfully listed some recently:

- The composite fuselage of a Boeing 787 is made all in one piece, obviating the need for thousands of fasteners. The weight of the aircraft has been cut by 20%.
- Making fan blades and fan cases out of carbon fibre composite materials has enabled Rolls-Royce to save 340 kg in engine weight.
- Electrically charging components before dipping them in a paint bath can save 40% of the weight of 4 million components on an Airbus 380.

The list goes on and on: from wings to tail skids, from seats to wheels, and even the pilot's 18 kg flight bag holding manuals and maps has been replaced by LED displays.

And we all know that it won't stop there; technological progress never does. When there is a Business imperative then progress results. Join that up to regulatory impetus from governments and people "doing (and being seen to do) the right thing" and that kid in a hut by the sea in Bangladesh might have a chance.

Because progress is being made; it ain't all bad.

## Reasons to be Cheerful

**"A pessimist sees the difficulty in every opportunity; an optimist sees the opportunity in every difficulty."**

**Winston S. Churchill**

The average American can expect to live 78.8 years. The average Brit does better than that at 81.2 years. That puts the British on a par with the Finns but behind the Luxembourgers. If you want to live longest, statistical averages will take you to Japan with an average life expectancy of 83.7 years, closely followed by Singapore and Switzerland, both over 83. The country where, on average, a human being will die earlier than anywhere else is Sierra Leone, where they just scrape past 50 years. When you reflect on the fact that a third of Americans are affected by obesity, a problem West Africa would love to have, it puts 50 playing 78 into context.

But everywhere, even in Sierra Leone, mankind is living longer year-on-year. With an occasional localised blip, even in developed countries, the trend is all one way and appreciably so over the past 30 years. Significant medical advances and better health education have made a major contribution. But the knock-on effect of Business investment in developing economies (employers need their workers to be healthy, literate and numerate and capable of getting to work along safe roads) is a huge factor. Business makes the difference.

- On 7 August 2016, high winds in Scotland meant that wind turbines produced enough to power the equivalent of all the electricity it required. Half of the UK's electricity was generated from low-carbon sources for the first time in the summer of 2016. And for four consecutive days in the summer of 2016, Portugal (yes, the whole country) ran on renewable energy alone.

- The world's largest marine protected area, in the Antarctic, has been created with the support of even the Russians.
- The world's wild tiger population has increased from 3,200 in 2010 to 3,890 in 2016 (a century ago there were 100,000).
- Nobody has poached a rhinoceros in Nepal for two years. A small achievement of course, but significant in many ways.
- And the giant panda population has increased by 17% to 2,000 over the past 10 years.

Why do these seemingly random facts matter? Because, as every Businessman and Businesswoman knows, without customer engagement you're nowhere. People have to see results; they have to think it's all worth it. Photogenic tigers and pandas are part of that initiative; it's no coincidence that the World Wide Fund for Nature chose a giant panda for its logo!

Interestingly, a lot of good work in conservation is being carried out by the oil and gas companies. So often public pariahs in the debate, they can stand tall in many areas. That old canard of the "general public hypocrisy" raises its head again whenever oil is mentioned. For some reason, many believe that BP shouldn't even be sponsoring the British Museum, and presumably the demonstrators who offensively lobbied for this decision used no fossil-fuel-generated energy in their homes or workplaces or in their children's schools or on their holidays! But so much technological advance is being made by oil and gas companies and so many conservation projects owe their very existence to them.

Business is key to saving mankind on this planet of ours. Every Business has a role to play and if we are serious about Fixing Business there can be few better areas where we can grasp the initiative, make a difference and be seen to do so than the environment and climate change. We should ignore the politically motivated and often misguided complaints of so many in the Green lobby and show by what we do, not by what prejudiced people think that we do, that we can make a difference and be a force for good in the world.

## Key Questions

- What have you done to lessen pollution in your Business?
- How are you saving water and energy in your operations or at home? Have you put a money's worth figure on this?
- Do you advertise what you're doing? Do your workforce and customers and local community know?
- Are you helping your employees get, and stay, fit? Do you provide routine medicals for them?
- Do you involve your supply chain, the local media and your MP in your initiatives?

# CHAPTER 6

# THE BOARDROOM: EXECUTIVE PAY AND THE GULF BETWEEN BIG AND SMALL BUSINESS

*"There is nobody in this Country who got rich on their own …
You built a factory out there; good for you. But … you moved
your goods to market on roads the rest of us paid for. You hired
workers the rest of us paid to educate. You were safe in your
factory because of police forces and fire forces that the rest of
us paid for. You built a factory and it turned into something
terrific or a great idea. God bless! Keep a hunk of it. But part
of the underlying social contract is you take a hunk of that and
pay forward for the next kid who comes along."*

—Elizabeth Warren

If we are truly going to Fix Business, if we are going to win hearts and minds, then we are going to have to address the elephant in the room: the boardroom. Perhaps more than anything else, what the boardroom does (or is perceived to do), what it decides (or is perceived to decide), and especially what it is paid has an effect on the perception of Business and its reputation.

We should accept that there are elements of wealth creation that the national psyche is just never going to accept. Someone sets up on their own, risks everything, borrows a lot and mortgages it all, rarely sees the family grow up as the Business is built, works incredibly hard, employs a lot of people, provides livelihoods for hundreds, pays a shedload in tax which makes a real contribution to providing schools and hospitals for the country, eventually sells out and puts a lot of money (after one more payment to the Inland Revenue) in the bank. Our hero buys a Rolls-Royce. It pulls up at the traffic lights in town one morning and people spit at it. "Rich bastard" and "capitalist scum" are amongst the nicer things that are shouted in the direction of the spittle. But someone who has never done a day's work in their lives wins the lottery one Saturday night and buys a Rolls-Royce. As it pulls up at the same traffic lights the winner is recognised: "good on yer, mate!" and "brilliant!" follow it down the street. Strange world!

We live in a world where so many parts of society complain (sometimes justifiably) about the levels of executive pay in

Business and politicians come up with policies to cap them, yet apart from a passing reference after a bad result, they leave the grotesque charade that is the pay levels in Premiership football alone. Fifty grand a week – a week! – for poor performance by a 23-year-old lad, and no one says a word. I once made this observation to my questioner who raised the issue after a speech I had delivered; he said that he could easily do the CEO's job, he just needed training, but he could never do the footballer's job since that talent was a gift! Wrong, probably on both counts in most cases, but a widely held justification for unfairness in condemning the one and not the other.

We must accept the Tall Poppy syndrome prevalent in many western democracies. Nurture and feed and encourage success until success arrives. Then when the poppy is taller than all the rest, regardless of actual (as opposed to perceived) behaviour, devote as much energy, bile and bitterness as possible to cutting the tall poppy down to the required size, whatever that may be.

But there is so much we could be doing! And a lot of it starts in the boardroom. Perhaps I should start by stating what I mean by that.

Thousands of small Businesswomen and Businessmen look at various aspects of corporate behaviour and do not recognise it at all. There are many ways (and I deal with several in this book) in which small Businesses can help Fix Business but the type of corporate behaviour I address here is not one of them. Indeed, such behaviour frustrates the hell out of small Businesses just as it does the general public. Moreover, they suffer from the bullying nature of big Business when a Group finance director proudly states to the board that a balance sheet can look better, so far as "cash at bank" or alternatively "overdraft" is concerned, by indulging in some "creditor stretch". A euphemism for unilaterally deciding that you can start banking with your small business suppliers rather than the bank. Don't dip into the bank account to pay the little guy; just let him be owed the money for a while longer and delay paying him … simply because you can. He won't want to lose your Business and couldn't afford to pay a lawyer to recover the sum due anyway, so just do it. To hell with the havoc on the small Business's cash flow that your decision will create; the sheer worry, the wages that might not get paid … and the consequent loathing of the big Business that ensues. We all had to deal with such behaviour in the playground when we were children; it's called bullying.

**"If your conduct is determined solely by consideration of profit you will arouse great resentment."**

**Confucius**

It is pointless creating Codes of Best Practice about this. They will be observed in the breach. It is a waste of time having implied terms and conditions in contracts that can be actioned by the victim; no one who wants to stay in Business will risk it, and the Big Fella knows it. I have concluded that the only way this cancer in the Business environment can be eradicated is if such behaviour (with some safeguards around verification and proper delivery) is individually criminalised. Nothing to do with recovery of the money owed; not a charge against the company but against the board of the miscreant, every member personally, executive and non-executive. Let's get this up there with corruption and breaches of health and safety regulations. It would not be up to a small Business to take action; criminal behaviour is for the police and the magistrates, not the civil courts. This would make such a difference to the supply chain, to investment and to efficiency. And if everyone had to do it (including the public sector who are not the world's speediest payers either) then nobody would get an individual advantage but the whole drive of wealth creation and employment and provision of working capital for more and better investment would make such a stepchange.

Big Business could do so much more with their supply chains to improve capital investment and upskilling and training. The Japanese auto sector taught the British motor industry an excellent lesson in this area. Don't beat up your suppliers on price whilst neglecting all the other aspects of what they do and how they do it. True partnering is essential to productivity enhancement and quality-based competitiveness. But do Tier Three and Tier Four suppliers practise this further down the chain? "Do as you would be done unto" is a maxim that should be followed in this field, as in every other walk of life. Moreover, the power of procurement by the public sector could be such a force for delivering improvement in productivity in the small Business supply base. So often the politically correct "thought police" make it a condition of a supply contract that standards of diversity in many forms are adhered to, but what about "I like your quality, I like your prices, now ... how do you skill and train your people?" What an enormous difference that would make, and it has to start in the boardroom of the big Business or the public-sector organisation.

But we must be grateful that the big Businesses are around; we need them! According to research conducted by PricewaterhouseCoopers, the overall tax contribution of Britain's largest 100 companies increased by 2.2% to £82.3 billion in 2016; that's paying for a lot of schools and hospitals! PwC found they spent £26 billion in capital investment during the year and £8 billion on research and development. The 100 largest companies produced 13.3% of all UK tax receipts. Their total tax rate (overall tax cost compared with profit) was 46.4% in 2016, up from 42.9% in 2015 and 38.2% in 2008. It might be an inconvenient truth for those who despise Business but those PwC figures speak for themselves; and, what's more, 6.6% of Britain's working population are employed by them as well.

So much of how our country pays its way in the world, its exports, come from the Big Fellas. Whether goods or services, they are sold around the world in highly competitive markets by our big companies. Their brands are world-renowned, their innovation, quality and value-added dimension are way ahead of many other countries' Businesses. And because the UK is such an open Business society and such a welcoming home for inward investment, thousands of big companies from all over the world have major bases in our country and export their goods and services around the globe.

Every small Business in the land should also be grateful that their big cousins are there in the economy, driving it on. For whilst it is true that national economic growth tends to come from the small and medium-sized Business sector, every member of that group depends in some way or other either on the public sector or big Business. And the public sector can only spend taxpayers' money and 13.3% of that comes from big Business!

## SO WHY DON'T WE LIKE THEM?

Fixing the reputation of Business, getting the small Business sector, the public sector, the voluntary sector, the media and the politicians to value, publicly, what wealth creation is all about and to start saying so, calls for one thing above all else: dealing with the excess and perceived (and often real) disproportionality of executive pay. This issue, above all else, is the drag anchor on any initiative to win the hearts and minds of the public as we try to Fix Business.

**"He who is not content with what he has, would not be content with what he would like to have."**

Socrates

137

Researchers at Lancaster University Management School found that pay for the chief executives of Britain's top 350 listed companies increased on average by 82% between 2003 and 2014 (many people will be surprised that the rate of increase is not more, but it is an average figure of course) whilst returns, using the most meaningful measure of value creation, improved by less than 8.5% over the same period. The average FTSE 350 boss is now paid £1.9 million per annum, up from £1 million in 2003. Where is the link between pay and value creation? Why isn't something being done about it?

The High Pay Centre claims that bosses of big companies were paid 47 times their average employee's wage in 1998; in 2014, it was 130 times as much! Employees no longer see the rewards from increased productivity as they should. The top 1% now take 95% of any gains; it was 50% 20 years ago.

Weijia Li and Steven Young at Lancaster University, whose research is so revealing, referred to "the illusion of pay-for-performance while failing to deliver the reality". Rewards have continued to escalate disproportionately because "simplistic metrics of short-term performance such as earnings per share growth and total shareholder return are the dominant means of measuring performance in chief executive remuneration contracts". They propose that a better measure is "economic profit" which measures the return a company makes against the cost of capital. If a company makes a profit that is lower than its cost of capital, it is effectively destroying value for its shareholders and creditors.

And guess what that well-known contributor to the debate, "a spokesman from the CBI", said by way of response? "Businesses shouldn't award exceptional pay for poor performance." He went on to tell us what bears do in the woods!

Philip Aldrick in *The Times* analysed the increase in CEO pay of five of the UK's flagship big Businesses and it makes alarming reading:

- Shell: 2005 £2.4 million, 2015 £4 million.
- HSBC: 2005 £2.5 million, 2015 £7.34 million.
- Unilever: 2005 £1.9 million, 2015 £7.7 million.
- BP: 2005 £3.3 million, 2015 £9 million.
- British American Tobacco: 2005 £2.1 million, 2015 £4.5 million.

Many fund managers and remuneration committees will take refuge in the justification that they are agreeing pay levels that are "the norm" or that "reflect the median of what the market is paying" or "we have taken professional advice on the subject". Would Bob Dudley at BP really "walk" if his pay last year had been less than £9,000,000? How many banks providing Stuart Gulliver with the style, brand, influence and location that HSBC does, would pay him £7.34 million? We need far more toughness about this in boardrooms, and more involvement by shareholders. The recent BP AGM saw a £5.2 billion loss reported to shareholders, with 7,000 job cuts and a 14% reduction in the share price somehow justifying a 20% increase in the CEO's pay to £14 million! Where was the shareholders' riot? What will it take for shareholders to make such behaviour the stuff of yesterday?

## SHAREHOLDER INVOLVEMENT

There has to be much more active shareholder involvement. The investment funds that constitute the bulk of UK plc shareholder base have, for years, been passive box-tickers on this issue. Whilst I appreciate that a lot of pressure is brought to bear on chairmen and CEOs in private, we badly need the whole issue dealt with out in the public gaze. Something must not only be done but must be seen to be done.

In November 2016, Hermes Investment Management called for a fundamental rethink in the way that top executives are rewarded. They took the view that bonuses should make up a much smaller proportion of total pay. (Indeed Neil Woodford, one of the great fund managers of the past few years, has abolished bonuses completely at his fund management and investment Business.) In addition, Hermes suggested that boards should also have total discretion to veto bonuses where the executive has on paper met targets but is still not regarded as deserving of the bonus the formula sets out.

Hermes further recommends that the chairman of a board's remuneration committee should be obliged to write to all staff every year explaining the basis for the CEO's pay and, crucially, put it in the context of wider pay in the company. Members of the board should also meet employees to discuss the CEO's pay and the ratio of CEO pay to median staff pay should be published. Saker Nusseibeh, chief executive of Hermes, said that boards struggling to justify a CEO's pay package to ordinary staff, including the lowest paid, should ask themselves why. He called for "much simpler, more transparent and less leveraged pay packages." "Fund managers," he said, "have the power and responsibility" to curb soaring pay "but have chosen not to use it."

## REFORM

If the essential key to Fixing Business is the wholesale, public, transparent embracing of socially inclusive wealth creation, then why not introduce the financial incentivisation of the CEO to deliver on other factors as well? Training; skills (not just in the Business but in the supply base as well); progress on medium to long-term investment programmes that yield no short-term reward but are essential for global competitiveness in this, Asia's century; delivery on environmental programmes and CSR projects; increasing liaison with schools, colleges and universities; and spending more on research and development. Bonuses and share awards keyed to development of the Business in the round as well as "doing the numbers" would fundamentally shift corporate behaviour and eventually public appreciation of Business.

It matters. Reform is urgently required. We are at five to midnight on this issue. If Business does not sort this out and be seen to do so, then others (especially that most dangerous of species, the popularity-hungry politician) will do it for us:

- Workforce representatives on boards might be a politically motivated trade unionist's dream but it would make a mockery of the board meeting; so much of what is discussed and reported on is confidential – you couldn't blame the Union Rep for sharing everything with her or his colleagues back at the ranch and then we'd all be reading the secrets of the Business in tomorrow's papers!
- Statutory caps on pay might sound workable but there would be ways of getting round them; the regulatory regime would create another mountain of red tape and the taxpayer (or yet another profit-sapping levy on the Business itself) would pay for that fully-paid-up visitor from the "Sales Prevention Team": the Government Inspector! So much time would be taken up on compliance rather than creating the wealth in the first place.

This simmering discontent is in grave danger of boiling over. We must start with a whole new set of criteria for additional rewards being established voluntarily by Businesses themselves. No more stupendous pay packets for less than stupendous performance. The last thing we need in the UK is to be rendered totally uncompetitive by having Business-ignorant politicians putting our house in order for us with ill-thought-through, playing-to-the-gallery legislation. In a globalised hunt for talent some CEOs would up sticks and take their chance in other countries, but hopefully many other countries would follow suit and Businesses around the globe are surely by now aware of the serious and cataclysmic discontent of the general public.

In 2012, Sir Roger Carr, Chairman of BAE Systems and then President of the CBI, said: "As Businesses and individuals, standards have been variable, greed prevalent and fairness forgotten in a number of sectors. No one should expect forgiveness from those [harmed by] the misdeeds of the powerful and the contemptible few."

In 2016, Paul Drechsler, Chairman of transportation group Bibby Line and then President of the CBI, said Business has become part of the "growing mistrust of big institutions" where Businesspeople are seen by the wider population as a "privileged few" who "don't look or sound like them and who seem to play by a different set of rules". He observed: "There have been unacceptable transgressions, which have made people question the value of what we do, and our right to do it."

What will the then President of the CBI be saying in 2020? Much the same? Oh, how I hope not. For then it will be too late!

**"What is infinite? The Universe and the greed of men."**
Leigh Bardugo

Wouldn't it be marvellous if part of the bonus of the CEO of a big Business was only paid provided that, within a five-mile radius of one big company operation in, say, five countries (definitely including the UK), adult illiteracy and innumeracy were abolished? We can no longer walk on by on the other side of the road; we cannot leave it to others. It *is* Business's responsibility (and I include the shareholders and the supply chain) and executive pay is where it begins and ends.

As I said on BBC Radio Four at the time of the controversy concerning Sir Philip Green's sale of BHS and the current state of the pension fund: "What do you want to be Philip? The richest guy in the graveyard?"

**"Doing nothing for others is the undoing of ourselves."**
Horace Mann

Of course there are many socialist members of parliament who say that the real answer to Fixing Business is to applaud small Business and take horrible big Business and nationalise it! For some reason, at a stroke, the problem goes away. This argument, promulgated seriously and often – and without a hint of irony – happily ignores two major problems at the outset:

- Small Businesses often become, whether by organic growth or merger/acquisition, big Businesses.
- In an integrated, ultra-competitive global economy, what do you do when the rest of the world isn't walking to the beat of the same drum?

But let us explore one example of where the socialist siren call to force through public ownership appears to have more acceptance amongst the general public than elsewhere: the railways.

Poor service in some regions, poor management in others, politically motivated strikes by trades unions causing widespread costly misery to hundreds of thousands … and apparently the universal answer is "take the lot into public ownership".

So:

- The country would sacrifice competition and choice to the most cumbersome monopoly on Earth: the public sector.
- The huge success of massive capital investment and customer-focused service over a quarter of a century that has put millions more people into use of the railways every day since privatisation would be ignored.

- So many of the operating problems of today's railway are caused by infrastructure issues and that side of things is already in public ownership!
- We should ignore that wherever competition has been allowed full rein (Chiltern Railways v Virgin serving the London–Birmingham requirement for example) the answer has been better service, enhanced value for money and increased usage.

Back in the mid-nineties, after privatisation, I remember asking the head of British Rail Midlands Region at the busiest interchange in the country, Birmingham New St, what was the biggest difference for him now that he was operating in the private sector. He said it was the fact that management of the railway no longer took place on the floor of the House of Commons and he could devote all his time to running the railway and not (at a moment's notice and with scant regard for the day job) having to frame answers for ministers at Question Time.

Why would anyone think that by the taxpayer owning the railway, and ministers and their civil servants ultimately managing it, things would be different? Would the unions suddenly stop trying to bring down the democratically-elected government? Would investment be greater when non-rail users have to pay for it as well as passengers? Would competition be allowed between two operations owned by the same entity?

Socialism and public ownership do not Fix Business and no matter how frustrating aspects of the train operations in the UK currently are, the nightmare socialist alternative of having politically-motivated, anti-wealth creation, competition-averse, big-spending politicians affecting to manage the railways would have been far worse.

The biggest wake-up call for the perceived elite that is big Business came in 2016 with the Brexit vote in Britain and the election of Donald Trump in the USA and I explore these in the next chapters.

## Key Questions

1. Do you know which companies your pension fund is invested in?
2. Have you asked your pension fund manager for details of the pay of the CEO of each company in which it is invested?
3. Have you asked him how it voted your stock regarding the CEO's remuneration and why?
4. Do you link actively with the supply chains of which you are part on issues other than price and delivery?

# CHAPTER 7

# DEALING WITH A POST-BREXIT WORLD

*"What separates the winners from the losers is how a person reacts to each new twist of fate."*

—Donald Trump

Saturday 25 June 2016 dawned bright and dry, and in the market square of Banbury in Oxfordshire the BBC had set up the red sofa for an outside broadcast edition of their Breakfast Show. It was some 27 hours since the country had voted by a sizeable majority (52%–48%) to leave the European Union. I was that morning's guest on the sofa in that market square, surrounded by the street traders preparing their stalls for the day. A small crowd, even at 8:20 in the morning, had gathered behind the cameras.

That morning, live on BBC1 television, I said something which produced the biggest mailbag (along with its electronic and digital versions) that I have ever had, of which over 90% was supportive of what I'd said. So many letters said thank you for clearly stating the positive way forward amongst so much establishment-driven pessimism. As I write this chapter in the first few days of 2017, it is worth looking again at what I said that day:

"I am a reluctant leaver; I wanted to remain in a reformed European Union but I had no confidence that Brussels would stop its march inevitably towards 1970."

"I am thrilled that, subliminally, almost subconsciously, the Great British Public have put their democratic freedom ahead of money."

"The establishment elite have had a kicking; trade unions, big Business, ministers, Brussels and the markets, every one of them tried to frighten the living daylights out of Britain for the past eight weeks, but the British public went to a secret ballot box and said: 'Know what? I like electing my leaders; I don't like being told what to do by unelected, unaccountable people so I'm getting out and if it costs me a few bob for a couple of years, so be it.'"

"The trouble is that the Remain Camp will be very sore, they're in shock and they will now threaten *Armageddon*. They will go into one Almighty Sulk."

"We are going into uncharted water; Business likes stability and it's going to be choppy water for weeks. The establishment elite are going to have to swallow a lot of humble pie but they will be in a Sulk. If they'd won they would have expected the losers to say: 'right, it's democracy, buckle down and make this happen for this wonderful country of ours. So the Remain Camp should bring their supreme talent, contacts, ability, money and make them work for our country. That's told Europe there's something more important than money; it's called democracy.'"

At this point the microphones picked up the crowd shouting "Hear! Hear!" I carried on:

"If this has been an important lesson for Brussels then I think it's a day's work well done."

> **"Brexit is an enormous, seismic shift in global everything."**
>
> Lord Digby Jones, 25 June 2016

"It is a golden opportunity; Britain is the most globalised country on Earth; we are an open society; we are not racist; we are a tolerant place to be. We have a golden opportunity to make Europe our friends, our partners, but in an environment where *all* the world is out there for us. We are going into the only race that matters in Asia's century: the global race."

> **"If we don't say full access to the internal market is linked to full freedom of movement, then a movement will spread in Europe where everyone just does whatever they want."**
>
> Angela Merkel, Chancellor of Germany, 6 October 2016

"To the Remain Camp, MPs, the media, Businesses and trades unions I say: 'Just understand that we can take this opportunity and our grandchildren will say thank you.' That's the challenge, now suck up democracy when it doesn't work for you and go and make it happen."

As the country heads towards the commencement of Brexit negotiations it is worth remembering my words that June morning; they are as relevant today as they were then. There are many MPs who have honed disingenuousness to a fine art: "Of course I will respect the democratic will of the British people, *but* ..." is their familiar refrain. They want us to remain in the Single Market and the Customs Union; they acknowledge that along with that state of affairs comes continued freedom of movement of labour (for which read "people") and continued submission of our judicial system to the one in Luxembourg. So they really want EU-lite.

## SO WHAT DID THEY REALLY WANT?

But, without doubt, whilst there are thousands of reasons as to why the 52% (or the 48% for that matter) voted the way they did one thing is certain. The 52% want the UK to take back control of its borders and its laws. I find it obfuscating to the point of deceit when Remainers respond to that observation by saying our country needs immigration (and the nation's darling is wheeled out as the example: "the NHS will fail to exist without immigration") and so free movement is OK. Of course we need immigration, but if we are going to win in the global race that is Asia's century we have to be able to take the number, the type of skill, the age of immigrant (genuine asylum seekers excepted of course) that suits the UK; control of one's borders does not mean no immigration, it does not mean anyone here needs to leave and it certainly does not mean any tolerance at all of disgusting, racist, bullying and offensive behaviour displayed by a small but vociferous minority. But it does mean that our population feels in control of its own borders again, and that feeling of loss of control is at the core of the Brexit vote.

> "The UK doesn't stop being a big European Partner."
>
> Antonio Costa, Prime Minister of Portugal, 11 October 2016

As I talked and listened to people all over the country during the referendum campaign (I campaigned to get back control of my country, not, as I told him to his face in private a few weeks before the vote, to make Boris Johnson Prime Minister) I formed the view that we have been a divided nation for some time and only a national exercise such as the vote on Brexit brought it to a head.

Benjamin Disraeli, the British prime minister in the 1860s, said of the Britain he governed: "Two nations between whom there is no intercourse and no sympathy, who are as ignorant of each other's habits, thoughts and feelings as if they were … from different planets."

London has made a considerable success of immigration; its hugely successful and world-class financial services sector is proof of that, as is its entire leisure, tourism and entertainment industry. But it doesn't look like a success if you live in many places in the North of England or in Wales. People there feel that no one is on their side, that they are powerless … and they had the chance to say so! In 1381, Watt Tyler led a Peasant's Revolt, full of violence and death, against the London-based establishment elite of the day. Nowadays, thank heavens, our mature democracy revolts in a peaceful way, but revolt there was, make no mistake. The chap in Hartlepool who said: "I'm told I will lose a lot if we vote to come out. I've got nothing to lose!" Or the worker at Nissan (partly owned by Renault and exporting the majority of the product to the EU) who said: "It's high time those people in London had a kicking; they have got to realise we matter as well!"

And they faced attitudes and facts which only endorsed their opinions:

- I was told in all seriousness by a senior accountant in London that he couldn't understand why such an important decision for the country was being left in the hands of unintelligent, poor people in the north of the country!
- The four leading members of the Labour Party front bench (Leader, shadow Chancellor, shadow Foreign Secretary and shadow Home Secretary) have contiguous constituencies in North and North-East London. No one in Blackburn is going to think they can empathise with them.
- The then leader of our greatest ally, which country's disastrous forays into recent wars have been fully supported by the UK with great loss of blood and treasure, told us that if we voted to leave then we could get to the back of the queue in trade talks! And what self-respecting American says "queue" anyway? Americans "wait in line"; we queue. I could be forgiven for thinking that Obama was put up to that by the Prime Minister; what I do know is that his statement acted as an effective recruitment sergeant for Brexit.

## THE UK SHOULD BE LEAVING THE EUROPEAN UNION, THE SINGLE MARKET AND THE CUSTOMS UNION AS QUICKLY AS POSSIBLE

**"We must try to formulate offers in a way so that the British remain close to us."**

Sigmar Gabriel, Minister for Economic Affairs and Vice-Chancellor of Germany, 6 October 2016

There are three distinct areas in this enormously important issue and each one matters to Business; Business can do much to help the country and itself by getting involved. Business optimism is good; as 2017 unfolds before us UK Business, large and small, is seeing annual GDP growth of around 1.75%, with the Bank of England and other ... er ... experts upwardly revising this to a figure beginning with a 2 already. In the six months since Brexit, our economy did not witness the plagues of frogs and locusts and death of the first-born that those experts predicted, and Business can see the remarkable resilience of the UK economy. We should make the most of every bit of good news, keep all our employees well-informed and work – in local communities as well as nationally and internationally – at changing the mood music away from that of those who are still in the GRS: the Great Remain Sulk.

The three areas are:

## 1. Brexit

The EU has to leave its emotional baggage at the door and negotiate in the best interests of the people of Europe, not the ideologues. Start thinking about how to get the millions who are out of work (especially those in Southern Europe) into work; open up; *reform*! Why should the provisions of a Treaty that worked for six countries in the impoverished, frightened, war-torn Europe of 1957 be fit for purpose in Asia's century, some 60 years on? Just because of slavish adherence? Because the establishment elite of Europe like it that way? How on earth is the EU going to afford pensions and welfare and healthcare for its population in 2060 if it doesn't change? The EU should see Brexit as one helluva wake-up call!

But instead we have Michel Barnier, the EU's lead Brexit negotiator, stating that the final deal "would have to be worse than EU membership". Why, Monsieur Barnier? Pour encourager les autres? Wasn't Europe divided by a wall only some 28 years ago, built by ideologues terrified of people leaving and intent on making sure the penalties for doing so were severe enough to discourage others? What are you frightened of Monsieur?

On 6 October 2016, the President of France, François Hollande, said: "The British want to leave and pay nothing. It's not possible. There must be a threat ... there must be a price." Why, Monsieur Le President? But I despair when the *Financial Times*, which has been chief cheerleader of the Remainers with the resultant loss of all objectivity, actually said in an article by Janan Ganesh on 6 December 2016: "[The EU] will do more to set the terms of Britain's extrication than Britain itself, which was always the best reason to stay"!! My exclamation marks not his.

I am delighted that Theresa May, the Prime Minister, has stated that, in the Brexit negotiations, no deal will be better than a bad deal. Shooting the EU negotiators' fox of the prize of Single Market Access, wrongly assuming in their arrogance that the UK will pay a lot and concede a lot to have it, the UK can concentrate on what is clearly in the interests of everyone in the EU, from the unemployed of Greece to the carworker in Sunderland, and that is economic growth for both sides. Surely EU ideology must not get in the way of that?! We must be confident (not arrogant, just confident) in our negotiations. With great respect to dear friends, we are not Norway, Switzerland or Canada; the European Union needs us just as much as we need them, whatever their bombast might suggest. Germany sells a million cars a year in the UK; any attempt to impose a tariff on a Jaguar made in Birmingham and being sold in the EU should be met by a similar tariff on every BMW, Mercedes, Audi, Porsche, Ford, Seat and Volkswagen made in Germany (or Slovakia or Poland or Spain for that matter) and sold in the UK. Making any of those cars, in one of their great markets of the world, more expensive than a rival made in the UK or Korea or Japan or the USA will have the CEOs and the trades unions knocking on the doors of Frau Merkel and Monsieur Barnier tout de suite! Similar stories exist for Italian luxury goods and French agricultural produce (so would Monsieur Hollande like to name "the price" he expects the French farmer to pay exactly?) We must bear this in mind as Frankfurt and Paris seek to hurt London in negotiations over the financial services market.

Surely what should prevail is what is best for those in work in the EU and, even more so, for those not currently in work. They matter more than the hurt feelings of the Brussels elite or the Paris or Berlin ideologues.

## 2. Trading Arrangements with the Rest of the World

The drivel that was (and still is in some quarters) heard about the UK turning its back on the world, about us becoming isolationist by voting to leave the EU, should be treated with the contempt it deserves. We should stride out confidently to forge the trading alliances that await us.

> "We must conceive of this whole Universe as one Commonwealth of which both gods and men are members."
>
> **Marcus Tullius Cicero**

This is Asia's time. Four of the seven billion people on the planet live there; the world's two most populous nations on earth are in Asia. The UK is well-known there, well-invested and known for being free marketeers seeking to knock down the protectionist barriers at every turn.

Our financial services sector needs more and better access to the 1.2 billion Indian population. India wants better access to our 65 million population for its agricultural produce. We would happily provide this access but EU protectionism (fanned by the staggeringly powerful agricultural lobby of France and Southern Europe) forbids it. Well now let's see what can be done.

At last UK Business can make a much greater difference in the area of overseas development. When I was Minister of State for Trade in 2007–08 I was so frustrated by the way in which the enormous opportunities for international trade to help developing economies were sacrificed on the altar of short-term domestic political advantage.

The EU isn't alone in such behaviour:

- Japan tariffs Vietnamese rice imports to protect its rice farmers! What? Industrialised, innovative, globally-engaged Japan?
- The USA, so very generous with overseas aid, prefers to give out American tax dollars in aid to countries whose cotton exports to the USA are tariffed into uncompetitive pricing to protect the American cotton grower. Letting the developing country's cotton industry grow and thrive will do more for the creation of a sustainable economy than the regular American overseas aid cheque, and the tax dollars should be used to skill up the people (and invest in the equipment) affected by the issue to lead them into value-added work which is globally competitive and can be exported to the improved cotton-based economies!
- The EU practises this myopic protectionism at every turn, much to the constant disapproval of a powerless Britain. The EU, driven by the all-powerful agricultural lobby, protects by tariffs its farmers from imports from India. So the UK's

financial services sector gets short change from India in seeking to operate there in India's hope of using this as leverage to get a good deal on agriculture. With agriculture representing only 4% of UK GDP we will be far more relaxed about imports from India in return for our financial services sector diving into the market provided by the second most populous nation on earth.

At last UK Business will be free to get into those economies, trade and invest and use Business as a highway to a more literate, numerate and peaceful world.

So many countries around the world are keen to "sign up" with the UK. I am confident that a Trump Presidency will lead the way. The United States will be a hard negotiator but, with four million Americans going to work every day for Businesses headquartered in the UK and the President being a supporter of Brexit, and given the existing trade that exists between us, I am confident a good deal can be done and done quickly.

But we must equip ourselves to be more globally competitive if we are to make the most of new trade deals:

- We must have post-EU replacement regulation that is acknowledged as putting the customer first. Big Business was seen as very much part of the establishment elite against which the public rebelled on 23 June 2016 and the disaffection from their customer base must be healed.

- Both Business and government must invest more (and more quickly) in technological progress (from universal super-fast broadband to high-speed railways). Artificial intelligence, micro-robotics and big data will change manufacturing processes completely; we must start in primary schools and not stop throughout our lifetimes. This train is definitely leaving the station and our country needs to be on it.

> "We should resist trying to impose baby boomer working models on Millennials who want to live and work differently. But we need to take seriously the concern that flexibility is a slippery slope towards less secure lives and exploited workers."
>
> Dido Harding, *Financial Times*, 26 November 2016

- We must embrace the digitalisation of our lives and especially of the workplace. This will lead to more industrial unrest in the public sector where politically-motivated, Luddite-minded trades unions will block every attempt to provide the taxpaying consumer with more for less. Mind you, when have you seen a trades union welcome any technological, innovative advance at any time, in any sphere? The nation cannot afford to slip backwards on this issue. But Business must be sensitive to the fact that they too are often seen as the very forces against which many voted when they voted for Brexit.

- Government needs to develop a fiscal strategy that stimulates international trade (ever mindful of World Trade Organization rules against tax subsidies, although we should look very carefully at what other major economies do in this area and leave our pride behind as we follow the example of others). Also, tax incentives on investment in the digital economy should be introduced. How about introducing Capital Gains Tax on some currently exempt assets (classic cars, vintage wine or certain forms of home ownership for example) and transparently ploughing the tax raised into programmes to ensure that the nation's appalling levels of illiteracy and innumeracy become a disgrace of the past. Our global future will need productivity to be enhanced at every turn, not hampered by having our hands tied behind our backs as we climb into the ring.

## 3. Immigration

Those of a politically correct disposition should look away now. The nation and Business would both benefit from a sharp statement of the bleeding obvious when it comes to approaching the post-Brexit world and immigration.

First of all, we are not alone. Britain hasn't suddenly become a country of rabid racists wanting to kick out everyone with a different coloured skin or a "funny-sounding" name. Virtually all developed countries (and a fair few developing ones) are experiencing problems in dealing with the greatest migration of peoples the world has ever seen.

The average Brit understands very well why immigration is to be welcomed. However, what he or she has a real problem with is:

- The sheer volume of immigrants concentrated in specific areas with little or no attempt at social, economic or educational integration.
- The speed at which this has occurred.
- Being called a racist or a bigot by the establishment or liberal elite for complaining about it. "They should come and live where I live" is an often-heard response to a "there, there" placatory few words from a South-East-based opinion former who presumably couldn't understand why the Midlander or Northerner took revenge in the Referendum.
- Being told how immigration is essential with no reference to volume or location, and being met (yet again) with the "Well I understand how there can be an issue *but* ..." response, which skates round the issue.
- Regardless of the real reasons (and the immigrant is definitely in no way to blame for this) there is a feeling that "They've taken our jobs." This conveniently ignores the fact that immigrants tend to work longer hours for less pay and are often far more skilled. In fact, they make a larger contribution to the national economy than many people whose grandparents were born here but these facts are not acknowledged and the muddle-headed perception has to be dealt with.
- The democratically-elected government in Britain not being in *control* of who enters the country.

Both large and small companies can do a great deal to help with this issue. Frances O'Grady, the General Secretary of the TUC, has rung a few alarm bells in their direction, and whilst her tone may be confrontational – some would say unnecessarily so – she is absolutely right about the essential tenet of her argument. She maintains that companies need to deliver for the benefit of local communities and not short-term foreign shareholders or else the situation with nationalism (not just in the UK but in the USA and Italy as well) will get worse. She has called for a new "bargain between labour and capital" to stave off social divisions and protect the rule of law.

If Businesses are seen to be overlooking "home-grown" prospective employees in favour of immigrant labour, if they do not invest in their communities and if (especially in the case of Businesses owned by overseas shareholders) they behave as though the people in the community are just another tradeable commodity, they should not be surprised if those same people rebel when they can. More Businesses voted to stay in the European Union than to leave but they got precisely what they didn't want partly because of this very issue.

The solution is in Business's own hands and can be fixed.

Fixing Business requires input from many sources but Brexit can provide the catalyst for changes

> **"Nearly half of all shares in Britain are held overseas and only for a matter of months on average. Unless our political representatives have answers for that, we could see feelings that are at least as intense expressed about the sense of wanting some control."**
>
> **Frances O'Grady, General Secretary of the TUC, December 2016**

in behaviour, the eradication of prejudice, a fundamental shift in how Britain is situated in the Business world and a change for the better in society. But all this will happen only if we listen, if we learn and if we are confident in this Brave New World.

## Key Questions

- Do you keep all your employees regularly informed on issues in your Business that Brexit may (or may not) be affecting such as exports, imports or demand?
- Will your recruitment policy be affected by any reduction in the availability of immigrant labour?
- Are you preparing the local community (especially schools and colleges) for your skilled labour requirements over the next few years?
- Are you investigating new overseas markets, outwith the EU?
- Are you confronting your importers with fresh competition rather than just accepting price rises ostensibly caused by exchange rate fluctuations?

# CHAPTER 8

# WHAT'S NEXT?

*"One of the fundamental questions of today's world is undoubtedly the question of equitable globalisation."*

—Janez Drnovsek, Prime Minister of Slovenia 1992–2002 and President of Slovenia 2002–2007

There are three pillars to 21st-century globalisation: the easy and society-changing movement of goods and services around the world, the shift of huge amounts of capital between nations and markets at the press of a button and the greatest migration of peoples the world has ever seen.

Quite how the developed world meets the challenges set by these enormous issues will define success – economic, political and societal – for hundreds of millions of people and indeed it may not be too alarmist to say that the way in which globalisation is handled will be the deliverer of peace or otherwise over the next hundred years.

## A TRUMP PRESIDENCY: KING CANUTE OR SAVIOUR?

> **"The term 'globalisation' is conventionally used to refer to the specific form of investor rights' integration designed by wealth and power for their own interests."**
>
> **Noam Chomsky**

Back in March 2016 I was lecturing on the West Coast of the United States. I devoted a lecture in the series to the American Presidential election; this was at a time when Donald Trump was not even sure of the Republican nomination and Hillary Clinton was being given a good run for her money by Bernie Sanders. After my lecture, many people approached me with their views; I always welcome this since it presents a wonderful opportunity to learn "on the ground" from "real people". One gentleman told me he was going to vote for Trump. He was clearly not a "blue-collared redneck from the mid-West" so didn't fit my stereotypical labelling of a Trump voter.

He said he had just retired from an investment bank in New York City. I asked which one. He said "Mine!"

Mind racing but working hard on maintaining my sang-froid, I asked him why on earth someone like him would contemplate such a thing. He replied: "Three reasons:

First, Trump won't be nearly as excessive in office as his rhetoric suggests – they won't let him – but he will get things done and we need that.

Second, he will shake up all that lot inside the Washington Beltway and, God, do they need a good shake!

And third, he ain't Hillary Clinton."

That was the day I knew that the Donald Trump would become the 45th President of the United States of America.

Business, especially big Business, indeed the policymakers of the very fabric of capitalism itself, had better understand just why Trump made it to the White House. If the 21st century is to work for successful wealth creation, if the reputation of Business is to be fixed, then lessons must be learned and reasons for why things happened not arrogantly decried but rather understood, acted upon and be seen to be acted upon.

According to some very interesting research by the McKinsey Global Institute:

- Before 2008, growth in Gross Domestic Product contributed about 19 percentage points to median household income growth in the USA. In the seven years after the 2008 recession that fell to just four percentage points.

- Between 65 and 70% of households in the USA (and 24 other advanced economies, interestingly: democratic establishment elites beware!) were in segments of income distribution whose real market incomes (their wages and income from capital) were flat or had fallen in 2014 compared with 2005.
- Longer-run demographic and labour trends will continue to act as a drag anchor on income advancement. Even if the US economy resumes its historical high-growth trajectory, they project that between 30 and 40% of the working population may not experience market income gains in the next decade if labour market shifts (such as workplace automation) accelerate.
- Twenty times as many single mothers in the USA were in the lowest income households as in the highest income ones. The real household income of single-mother households declined nearly one percentage point more quickly than all other households in the decade between 2003 and 2013.
- More than half the respondents to their survey (in Italy, the UK and the USA) agreed with the statement: "The influx of foreign goods and services is leading to domestic job losses." They were also more than twice as likely to agree with the statement: "Legal immigrants are ruining the culture and cohesiveness in our society."
- Between 1980 and 2010, competition for low- and medium-skill jobs became global, with 85 million workers in emerging economies joining the labour force in export-related activities.

- Business has a role to play in helping to create solutions to this situation. Boosting productivity, GDP growth and employment, and enabling employees to find better-paid work are amongst their recommendations. Technology has skewed labour demand. In both manufacturing and services, robots and computers have automated tasks that once required workers, whilst staggeringly speedy information technological advance has streamlined Business processes and built new types of organisations that require less but more highly-skilled labour.

There is an element of "Stop the world, I want to get off!" in the democratic response of the American electorate to this situation but objectively you can see why it happened:

- They never took Trump's rantings and disgusting excesses seriously. The media did, which gave Trump all the column inches and air time he needed, and for free!
- Clinton represented everything that those who were at their collective wits' end despised: more of the same that, in their eyes, clearly hadn't worked; the political class, the elite with a sense of entitlement (Bill Clinton even stood on the platform at his wife's adoption as nominee and said: "It's your turn now") and a "nanny knows best" patronising attitude that their's was the only way.
- They had a genuine feeling that their world was slipping like sand through their fingers and Trump represented a last hope

who might just have the answer when all else had seemingly failed. As a woman who approached me at another of my pre-election lectures in America responded to my question "Why Trump?": "Given the mess we're in, why not?"

## So What Will a Trumpian Presidency Mean for Business on Both Sides of the Pond?

**Patient to dentist, as the drill starts up but the patient's hand is placed strategically between the dentist's thighs: "Now we're not going to hurt each other, are we?!"** In the first few days of 2017, the Ford Motor Corporation announced it had scrapped plans to build a $1.6 billion-dollar car plant in Mexico in favour of creating 700 new jobs in the USA. It will instead invest $700 million over the next four years to expand its factory in Flat Rock, Michigan to develop electric and self-driving cars. Mark Fields, the CEO of Ford, said that the company was "encouraged by the pro-growth policies that President-Elect Trump and the new Congress have indicated that they will pursue … We believe that these tax and regulatory reforms are critically important to boost US competitiveness and … drive a resurgence in American manufacturing and high-tech innovation."

In the last month of 2016, the air conditioner manufacturer Carrier decided to keep approximately 1,000 jobs in Indiana, cancelling plans to close a plant and move the jobs to Monterrey in Mexico, being persuaded by tax incentives to stay.

**"If someone can persuade Business to save or create 1,700 jobs in a month and he isn't even in power yet…!"** The ordinary person in Main Street is the beneficiary and Trump's constant tweeting and other astute use of social media connects him or her directly into the thought process and the result. Simple but very clever, and if Business goes about what is tantamount to a revolution in the right way then everyone is a winner and the reputation of Business can start to be mended.

But … what Trump's America has to contend with is something they have studiously ignored for over a decade: that globalisation is not Americanisation. Thomas Friedman's work in the late nineties was based on the premise that those two terms were synonymous and millions agreed with him. Wrong! Trade and inward investment is a two-way street; China and the USA are the dentist and the patient (it doesn't matter who plays which role) and a getting-richer China (its economy grew at close to 6.5% in 2016 and is projected to do much the same in 2017) will increasingly become a customer for American value-added goods and services with Uncle Sam not just being its customer. This is not the time for Trumpian rhetoric to put up the trading shutters; Business suffers and their employees suffer.

Those 700 jobs in Michigan will not be low-skilled jobs yet so many of those who feel left behind will not have the skills Ford need.

There is a win-win here for Business:

- The US economy was gathering momentum already, before Trump's election: a great base for a fiscal boost.
- Growth in jobs will be further stimulated by the good old-fashioned indulging in Keynesian spending on America's infrastructure.
- Trump should be spending American tax dollars on vastly improving the human infrastructure as well. Upskilling the Nation is *the* way to "make America great again". Then those 700 skilled jobs will be filled by people who thought all this had passed them by and that they'd been forgotten.
- The new President has two tendencies that can be turned to advantage for both Business and the country:
  1. He is an excellent communicator with the people who matter in this situation: the ordinary guy, the "left behind", or as Hillary Clinton called them, "the deplorables".
  2. He is a Businessman and is goal-focussed; indeed, he may well get so frustrated by the Beltway Process that he "signs out" and becomes even more unpredictable than he is already. That would be very dangerous, especially in foreign policy issues. But as a results-orientated person, he will do what has to be done and quickly (I think it might well be called "cutting the crap"!) to force things through.

If Business can be seen to be on the side of the ordinary guy helping these things happen, then "the Fix" just got a whole lot easier.

Business in the UK will benefit from the American stimulus. Four million Americans go to work for British companies operating there and the USA is our greatest trading partner. But we should definitely fear Trump's inherent protectionism. It doesn't take much to tip America into isolationism; I am always frustrated by the average American's belief that they are the Home of the Brave and the Land of the Free; brave they are, but free? In trade they are not, and yet they feel there is nothing wrong with being free to export everywhere else, which is strange.

The other cause for concern for UK Business with a Trump presidency is the effect his trade policies will have on international trade generally. We are such a globally-engaged nation that we would be hurt if various countries faced with Trumpism were to put up retaliatory barriers. But there should be two responses to that … speedily pursued:

- With a relatively low exchange rate UK Business should export like never before, to every nation on the planet but especially the USA. The substantial uptick in manufacturing export figures in the last quarter of 2016 should be built on.
- We should work on trade deals with every non-EU country, in confidence and indeed in secret if necessary. There are so many countries just aching for better trading terms with us as an independent country than they can have with us as

subservient to a protectionist EU. If Trump makes life difficult for these countries around the world, then we can offer a
(smaller but perfectly formed) alternative.

Lastly, a warning to Business. Do not listen to those civil servants who tell us (in resignation letters and the rest) how difficult all this is, and is going to become. They are so often
fully paid-up members of the Sales Prevention Team. When I
was Minister of State for UK Trade and Investment I was often
treated to the inside view when ministers basically followed
blindly what their civil servants advised. I often asked who was
actually running the country!

**Trump will be worryingly unpredictable in foreign policy, and "Engage Brain Before Opening Mouth" is a maxim he should tweet to himself every night.**

In telling the establishment elite that things *will*
happen, that goals *will* be achieved and that they
can tear up the old way of doing things, The
Donald may well be onto something. Remember
the "man who owned the bank" who said he was
going to vote for him? "He'll get things done," he
said. Well, if we believe in ourselves (instead of following that Thatcherite fear the Foreign Office have
believed for decades that they are there to super-
vise the decline of Britain) then we can have a
results-focussed decade as well … hopefully without all the Trumpian baggage that is so off-putting in so many
ways.

## NEXT STEPS

Over the next few years the political divide in the UK will be defined less by which party one belongs to or is inclined to vote for and more by whether one was part of the 52% or the 48%. This is worryingly divisive, but provides a massive opportunity for Business to boost the nation's morale, to show leadership and to explore new opportunities, to reach out to communities that are worried or confused and to show just how globalisation *can* be a force for good:

- Stop whingeing! This "blame Brexit for everything" has to end and quickly.
- Keep the pressure on government to recover full control of immigration so that Business can dip into a global rather than an exclusive EU reservoir of talent.
- Communicate with workforces and the media so that everyone knows that there is nothing wrong with belonging to a club, indeed many different clubs, but it all depends to which club you choose to belong. Over 54% of all UK exports go out with the EU. The EU's role in the world is shrinking, so why be exclusively tied to a sinking ship?
- Big Business liked the cosy Brussels world. Regulation (formulated by the influence of thousands

**"When you refuse to accept that globalisation in its current form has left too many people behind, you are not sowing the seeds for its growth but for its ruin. When you fail to see that the liberal consensus that has held sway for decades has failed to maintain the consent of many people, you're not the champion of liberalism but the enemy of it."**

Theresa May, Prime Minister of the United Kingdom, 14 November 2016 of lobbyists they paid for) was fixed to help them, with the interests of the small Business left to go hang. British SMEs will be free of those chains; make the most of it!

- Going "local" with the application and perceived benefits of globalisation can only be achieved by Business. The economic and social benefits of Business are not just for the metropolitan professional classes; how Business invests, where they invest and what they look for from that investment will define success in the battle to make globalisation relevant to everyone.

## There Are Some Things You Cannot Change ...

**"God, grant me the serenity to accept the things I cannot change, courage to change the things I can, and wisdom to know the difference."**

**Reinhold Niebuhr, 1934**

Any attempt "to do something about it" and try to Fix Business has to come to terms with a few reality checks:

- Changing cultures or national behaviour makes turning around a quarter-mile-long supertanker doing 12 knots in the crowded English Channel on a stormy day look easy!
- Politicians are short-termist by nature and also by survival instinct. So much of what needs to be done is either below the "appreciation radar" or is about avoiding short-term unpopularity despite any long-term benefit.
- There is a basic human envy upon which anti-Business party politicians ply their trade with some success. If you have

winners in society you will, by definition, get losers. And Business so often gets the blame, sometimes justifiably but often not.

- A compensation culture has become endemic in our society, where someone must be blamed for everything that goes wrong, where there is always a victim whose plight is played up by the media striving to fill the airwaves and the pages on a 24/7 basis, which leads inexorably to blaming Business. They're the ones with apparently deep pockets, they're the ones who are apparently driven only by profit and they're the ones who are up there ready to be shot down.

- There will always be bad Businesspeople. Business is only a reflection of society; there will always be bad teachers, bad policemen, bad politicians and (dare I say it?) bad journalists. But each revelation of a "wrong 'un" is a serious setback to the quest for Fixing Business and angers and disheartens the thousands who "do it right".

> **"Democracy is the worst form of Government apart from all the others."**
> **Sir Winston Churchill**

## There Is Much to Be Optimistic About ...

The forces of moderation are still to the fore in the Developed World; Austria did not fall to the Far Right, two million more Americans voted for Hillary Clinton than Donald Trump, the average Brit or German did not pick up a pitchfork and look for a convenient spike upon which to put a politician's head.

> **"We are all in the gutter, but some of us are looking at the stars."**
> **Oscar Wilde, "Lady Windermere's Fan"**

Even the most hardened Remainer must admit that the good old British economy has proved remarkably resilient since that Day of Revolution in June 2016.

According to research by *The Times* on 31 December 2016:

- A net 342,000 more people were in work at the end of 2016 than at the end of 2015.
- 74.5% of all 16–64-year-olds were in work in the middle of 2016, an all-time record.
- There were 103,000 fewer people (1.62 million) unemployed in the UK on 31 December 2016 than at the end of 2015.
- Output per hour worked is now (just) higher than it was before the 2008 crash; at last!
- Growth in GDP (at 2.2% for 2016) happened for the seventh successive year and the UK had the fastest growing economy in the G7.
- Average weekly earnings were £507 per person in October 2016, 2.6% higher than a year earlier.
- The FTSE 100 index ended the year at a new high, at 7142.83, up 14.4% in 2016, outperforming European indices by a big margin. Good for all our pension funds whose values have increased.
- 216,000 was the net number of additional Britons saying at the end of 2016 that they are very satisfied with their lives compared with a year earlier.

- The National Living Wage was introduced on 1 April 2016 meaning a compulsory pay rise for the 1.6 million lowest-paid workers in the country – that's 6.7% of all employees over 25. But of course those on pay levels just above the lowest-paid immediately required their pay differential to be maintained and so up went their pay, which in turn caused the next level up to want their differential to be maintained ... and so on all the way up the payscales of Business. So the lowest-paid 25% of the workforce (6 million workers) received a rise in their pay. Most Businesses took the hit in profit reduction rather than passing the cost onto the customer (but will presumably receive no thanks for that) and thus the rise was not inflationary. Good news! But remember that some of the biggest employers of the low-paid are the public sector so they can't pass on the additional cost (other than by looking for more from the taxpayer) so productivity enhancement has to be the number one priority.

So things are not as bad as some would have us believe. That provides Business with every reason to invest more in better kit and in skilling the workforce and begin all those corporate social responsibility initiatives that were considered unaffordable.

The past 25 years have delivered "the first reduction [in global inequality] since the Industrial Revolution" according to the

World Bank. Indeed the global average GDP per person in the 20 years before 2008 grew by 24% but this is an average and such a rise was not uniformly enjoyed; the lower middle classes of the developed world did not see such a rise in the reality of take-home pay and so a small rise for them, "the squeezed middle of our society," felt like retreat. Politicians didn't help; insufficient funds were directed to upskilling and retraining as low-skilled jobs migrated to Asia. Investment in people is the only answer, and then doing it again ... and again. Business is on the front line of this one and in the Fixing Business project there will rarely be an easier goal if sustained will and profit reallocation are present.

So, as I close my examination of the opportunities and challenges in Fixing Business, let me leave you with two ideas that are worthy of consideration:

## Overseas Aid

The Cameron coalition government committed the UK to spending 0.7% of national income (about £12.4 billion in 2016) on overseas aid. Per capita we are the most generous country on earth. Yet the average person in Britain (generous to a fault every time there is an appeal to help in time of disaster anywhere in the world) is left with the feeling that such generosity is being abused, that we are being ripped off:

- We gave China (yes, China, one of the largest economies on the planet, if not the largest) £40,000 to improve its copyright laws.
- The Chinese have also received £102,762 to promote a public-private partnership for the building of hospitals in Zhejiang, with no tie to this aid (God forbid we should hand out our cash in the same way as the Americans or the French or the Japanese) so other countries will get the resulting jobs.
- We gave £5.2 million to an Ethiopian girl band!
- We spent £285 million on an airport in St Helena that has been constructed in such a way and in such a location that it can't actually be used by aircraft! And the boss of the department that did this received a knighthood in the 2017 New Year's Honours List.

The list goes on and on. The generous British public are made to feel like suckers and the whole concept is brought into disrepute.

So why not hand the entire management of the distribution of this aid to UK Business who would agree to manage it for free? They have the expertise (civil servants clearly don't) and they have the "value-for-money" ethic. It would be a massive declaration of change in how Business sees its role in the world and it could link up with charities and governments in much the same way as it forges supply chains already. The rules of engagement would be formulated by a group of charities and civil servants, in consultation with Businesses and other deliverers, reporting to elected government (it's our money after all) and annual inspections and transparent reports. There would be a lot of scepticism at first but if Business is really serious about changing people's perceptions, then how about it?

**"If nothing is done then the whole project will fall into such disrepute that the real cases of need in our world will go without … and that would be a real disaster."**

The balance between development aid and the representation of our country abroad through the various channels available to government, including the Foreign Office, needs to change. We must not become an impotent empty vessel overseas, seen as a soft touch for free, no-strings money. The Foreign Office has over 160 missions abroad run at a cost to the UK taxpayer of £650 million a year. The budget for the Department for Foreign Development Aid is £12 billion! We give more every year just to Ethiopia and Pakistan than we spend on our entire diplomatic service. This just cannot go on. Britain's post-Brexit position in the world demands a fully tooled-up and confident Foreign Office; surely the days of seemingly buying nice thoughts about us through giving money to China are over?

## The NHS

In these closing pages there is no inclination on the part of the author to parade the good and bad aspects of this national treasure. Suffice it to establish common ground in observing that we can't go on as we are, and that more money on its own, without reform, won't fix it.

So here is an innovative idea to help both the country and the reputation of Business at the same time.

An area's NHS Trust will be chosen as a pilot and will be run entirely by Business; hospitals (all provision from A&E to geriatric, from elective surgery to cancer and heart treatment), including social care as it affects bed provision, procurement … the lot! But before the socialist ideologues scream "privatisation" it should be pointed out that the Business appointed to do this and handle the settled budget (and it may be a group of smaller local Businesses or a couple of larger ones or just one big one) will be doing it entirely for free! Yes … for nothing, zilch, zero, nil.

Various aspects of the daily delivery by the NHS would be made the responsibility of Business. The essence would be how to improve performance, cut out waste, enhance the patient experience and speed up processes. Hundreds of Businesses would be involved, many of them at a localised level in just one hospital, bringing their expertise to benefit everyone … for free!

How can a socialist complain if the skill and expertise of Business is brought in to benefit the NHS for nothing; no privatisation, no profit, just Business being used as an agent for the improvement of our society at no cost? What a massive contribution to the community that would be. The Business could afford it if handled correctly (after all, it would only involve a small part of each Business's operations and could become some of the best marketing they have ever done) and only in one area and maybe, just maybe, society would come to appreciate Business more and Business would see a role for itself in distributing the benefits of its wealth creation more immediately and directly.

**"After all, this is a time for a new way of looking at things, for delivering on changed parameters, for having everyone feeling Business is for them and that the benefits of globalisation have not passed them by."**

The Business that does this may see its cost as additional taxation; so be it. At least they will have more direct influence on how their taxed profits are spent than is currently the case ... and the goodwill created will be tangible, whilst the payment of corporation tax is not. No one could accuse Business of avoiding payment of this tax. It's their expertise and management that they're bringing to the party, not just their money. There would be many businesses combining together in one area. Business working for their local community at no charge – unbelievable! But then it's time we believed that anything is possible.

Business is in the last chance saloon as far as its reputation is concerned and yet the solutions, the ability to Fix Business, are in the gift of the Businesses themselves. Brexit and Trump create challenges but also opportunities. Education and training is such a great way of reaching out by Business into the lives and hopes of those who thought the benefits of Business had passed them by. We must be courageous in dealing with environmental issues and executive pay. We must think out of the box with some of the innovative ideas that have been the hallmark of quality Businesses over the centuries, as we search for ways to take the whole of society with us as we go about creating wealth.

Rarely has the developed world been so socially divided; yet one of the greatest potential agents of harmonisation, of whole communities developing self-respect, of people feeling they matter, is Business.

Through Fixing Business we fix many of society's problems ... and that can't be a bad thing, can it?

# ACKNOWLEDGEMENTS

E veryone knows that no book just writes itself and this one is no exception.

I thank my long-suffering Business Manager, Lorraine Ellison, for her multi-faceted dedication to the task of bringing my efforts to publication and for her help and support throughout this and many projects.

Thanks to my PA, Joanne Lowe, for unwaveringly keeping the show on the road over so many years.

Thank you to Jeremy Kourdi for giving some early structure and form to my idea for this book.

Thank you to Annie Knight, Pete Gaughan, Tessa Allen and Caroline Quinnell at Wiley for all their help, guidance and support in taking my idea to market.

# ABOUT THE AUTHOR

**L**ord **Digby Jones** is a crossbench peer in the UK House of Lords and also a well-respected advocate for Business. Former Minister of State for UK Trade & Investment in 2007–08, he was and is still the only Minister never to have joined the party of Government and is often heard to say "Business is my Constituency".

A former corporate lawyer and Director General of the Confederation of British Industry (2000–06), he speaks around the world on all aspects of Business, including the wider political and societal scene. He has presented a BBC 2 TV Series *New Business Troubleshooter* and is a regular commentator across the international media, appearing regularly on TV, radio and in the newspapers, where his views and opinions find a regular audience.

Born in Birmingham and educated through a Scholarship at Bromsgrove School, Digby Jones joined the Royal Navy before graduating from University College London and joining the law firm, Edge & Ellison, rising from Articled Clerk to Senior Partner. In 1998 he joined KPMG as Vice-Chairman of corporate finance, before taking up the role at the CBI.

In 2006 he was knighted for his services to Business and became Sir Digby Jones in the Queen's New Year's Honours List. In 2007 he became a Life Peer taking the title Digby, Lord Jones of Birmingham Kb.

His first book, *Fixing Britain: The Business of Re-shaping Our Nation*, was published by Wiley in 2011.

Lord Digby Jones holds a number of non-executive roles, chairing several Boards including Triumph Motorcycles, Thatchers Cider, Celixir plc, as well as senior advisory roles with Babcock International, Argentex llp, AON and Unipart. He is also a non-executive director of Leicester Tigers Rugby Club.

Digby believes passionately in the upskilling and lifelong training of communities. He is involved with several charities including Cancer Research UK, the Royal Navy & Royal Marines Charity, and Ladies Fighting Breast Cancer. He lives in Warwickshire with his wife, Pat, and enjoys rugby and military history. He is a past winner of *BBC TV Celebrity Mastermind* and is a major supporter of the Royal Shakespeare Company and the City of Birmingham Symphony Orchestra.

# INDEX

# INDEX

# INDEX